At the Foot of the Lud

A History of Luddenden Foot

by Sheena Ellwood

RP

Published by Royd Press
The Book Case
29 Market Street
Hebden Bridge
West Yorks.
HX7 6EU
www.bookcase.co.uk

Front cover photo: in 1935 villagers in Luddenden Foot
celebrated the Silver Jubilee of King George V.
Reproduced with the kind permission of Owen Sellers.

Cover design: Kate Claughan

ISBN: 978-1-907197-05-5

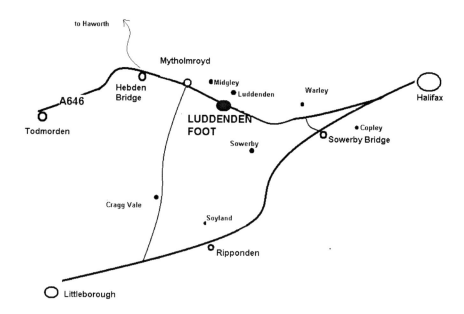

Luddenden Foot in the Calder Valley

Acknowledgements

For guidance I used David Dymond's *Researching and Writing History, A Guide for Local Historians* (Carnegie Publishing Ltd). I want to thank Owen Sellers for the chats we had about Luddenden Foot and for allowing me to use some of his father's photographs (J. T. Sellers). He also lent me a copy of the "Victory Souvenir Programme, Luddenden Foot Citizens' Social Week". Without his local knowledge this book would not have been possible. Garry Stringfellow told me about knurr and spel. Thank you to Elsie and Lesley Helliwell for sharing their memories of Luddenden Foot. Robert Huck kindly lent me his copy of Joseph Greenwood's "Jubilee of the Luddenden Foot Industrial Co-operative Society Ltd. 1860–1910". Greenwood's book was fundamental to an understanding of how the village developed and I have made many references to it. Thanks to Mary and Cyril Charnley who talked to me about their memories of Luddenden Foot. Many thanks to Jill Smith-Moorhouse, chair of Luddenden Foot Community Association, for her advice and for introducing me to Mrs M. Clay and Mrs A. Whitworth. Thank you also to Pauline Kenyon and Maggie Norton; also to Frank Woolrych and Issy Shannon for their help in tracing photos.

CONTENTS

Illustrations   vi
Maps   vii
Photographic acknowledgements   viii
The Luddenden Foot area   x
1. From cottage industries to the factory system   1
2. Poverty, petitions and rioting   14
3. Education, self help and co-operation   24
4. The Luddenden Foot Local Board of Health.   42
5. Towards the twentieth century   54
6. The village between the wars   65
7. Luddenden Foot's war effort   85
8. The clearances   95
9. The future   106

Abbreviations   112
Bibliography   112

ILLUSTRATIONS

1. Sheep gave the weavers their raw material — 1
2. The aqueduct carrying the Rochdale Canal over the Lud — 5
3. The small round house at Tenterfields — 7
4. Branwell Bronte statue — 17
5. The Burnley Road entrance to Methodist chapel — 18
6. The archway entrance to Cooper House mill — 25
7. Luddenden Foot's Congregationalist Chapel — 32
8. Boulder Clough Chapel — 32
9. Luddenden Foot Co-op Committee members in the 1860s (1) — 36
10. Luddenden Foot Co-op Committee members in the 1860s (2) — 38
11. Denholme Cottages, later renamed Co-operative Buildings — 39
12. The Victoria Hotel — 45
13. St Mary's church — 46
14. Luddenden Foot Co-op, High Lee Green, 1872 — 48
15. Luddenden Foot Co-op, 1910 — 49
16. Built in 1882, the bridge over the Calder at Luddenden Foot. — 50
17. Page from an 1884 almanac — 53
18. Denholme Mill from Burnley Road — 58
19. Denholme Mill from the Rochdale Canal bank. — 58
20. Co-op branch at Friendly, 1910 — 60
21. Co-op Jubilee Committee, 1910 — 60
22. The cenotaph in Holmes Park, Luddenden Foot. — 63
23. The inscription on the Luddenden Foot cenotaph — 63
24. Hellewell's Mill under construction, from the top of the mill chimney – 66
25. Hellewell's Mill under construction, from Railway Terrace — 67
26. Hellewell's new boiler at the base of the mill chimney — 68
27. Hellewell's Mill from Burnley Road opposite the Black Lion pub — 68
28. One of Hellewell's spinning sheds decorated for Christmas, 1930s — 69
29. Hellewell's prize-winning wagons, 1930s — 69
30. The fire at Hellewell's Mill in 1935 — 70
31. A new boiler arriving by train for Fairlea Mill, 1930s — 71
32. The boiler being manhandled into the boiler room — 71
33 Showing Luddenden Foot Mill at the bottom of the village, 1930s — 73
34. Traffic accident on Burnley road in Luddenden Foot, 1930s. — 73
35. Sewage works — 74
36. The Mechanics' Institute, now the Civic Centre, Luddenden Foot — 75
37. Warley Wood estate — 77
38. Smith's butchers, Denholme Buildings, Luddenden Foot — 79
39. J. T. Sellers' business card — 79
40. The Woodman Inn, Luddenden Foot — 80
41. Luddenden Foot AFC 1923-4 — 81
42. Garden Party in 1924 at Styles Farm — 82
43 Luddenden Foot Boy Scouts on the canal bank near Longbottom's Mill — 83

44. Holmes Park, Luddenden Foot, in 1935   84
45. Holmes park paddling pool. 1930s   84
46. Children at Boys Scarr in the inter-war years, in front of the sweet shop   85
47. Special Constables in Luddenden Foot   87
48, 49. Special Constable Identity Card   88
50. Air Raid Warden's notes about how to handle an incident, 1943   88
51. Luddenden Foot railway station, around 1940   91
52. Luddenden Foot's Victory Souvenir Programme   93
53. Saint Walburga's Amateur Dramatic Society Production   95
54. Luddenden Foot village when there were no concerns about road safety   97
55. Houses were cleared along the length of one side of Burnley Road   100
56. Tenterfields Business Park   103
57. Easter bonnet competition at Whitworth's Longbottom Mill   106
58. Staff at Luddenden Foot Co-op in the 1950s   107
59. Kershaw House Estate   108
60 Kershaw House Estate and the top o'Denholme area   109
61. Burnley Road Council School   110
62. "Isabel" travelling towards Luddenden Foot   111

MAPS

Luddenden Foot in the Calder Valley   iii
The Luddenden Foot Area   vii
Fulling mills in Luddenden Foot   3
Small mills on the Sowerby Hillside (18th century)   6
Mills in Luddenden Foot 1800-1830   9
Luddenden Foot village in 1841   15
Mills owned by the Whitworths in the 1860s   24
Luddenden Foot village in 1861   27
Friendly 2010 (Warley Grammar School)   30
Mills owned by the Clay family in the 1890s   56
Luddenden Foot mills in the 1930s   70
Luddenden Foot in WWII   89
The clearances   99
Traffic problems in the village centre   101

Photographic Acknowledgements

Author: 1, 2, 4, 5, 6, 7, 8, 16, 18, 19, 22, 23, 35, 36, 47, 48, 49, 55, 56, 59, 60, 61, 62.
Owen Sellers: Front Cover, 12, 13, 24, 25, 26, 27, 28, 29, 30, 31, 32, 34, 37, 38, 39, 40, 41, 42, 43, 44, 45, 46, 50, 52, 57.
The Co-operative Group: 9, 10, 11, 14, 15, 20, 21.
Issy Shannon: 17, 33, 54.
Elsie Helliwell: 53, 58.
Alice Longstaff Gallery Collection, BT 203: 51.
Private collection: 3.

Maps, drawn by the author, are not to scale.

"Wondrous is this wall-stone; broken by fate, the castles have decayed; the work of giants is crumbling."

Anglo-Saxon poem "The Ruin", trans. R. K. Gordon

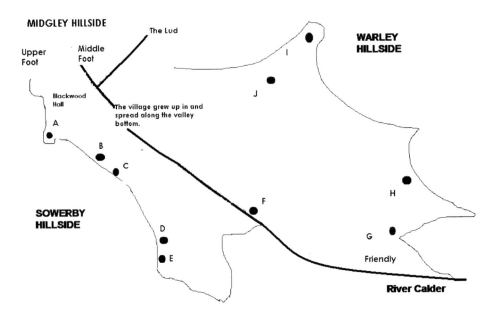

The Luddenden Foot Area[1]

The "Luddenden Foot area" means that area which in 1868 became the Luddenden Foot Local Board of Health District. One part of the "Luddenden Foot area" lies under the Sowerby hillside, with the other parts lying under the Warley hillside and to a lesser extent under the Midgley hillside. Before 1868, these three parts of the area were administered by the townships of Sowerby, Warley and Midgley.

Within the "Luddenden Foot Area" is the actual village of Luddenden Foot.

- A   High Lee Green
- B   Row End
- C   Lane Side
- D   Acre
- E   Boulder Clough
- F   Longbottom
- G   Row Pickle
- H   Hoyle House
- I   Shepherd House
- J   Butts Green

[1] O S map 1888-1893 LF LBH ccxxx, Halifax Library

Chapter 1
From cottage industries to the factory system

In the Middle Ages cottagers in the Calder Valley lived on the hillsides where they'd cleared away the trees to farm the land. The trees they cleared in the Luddenden Foot area belonged to three woods: Black Wood, Sowerby Wood and Warley Wood.[1] Above the clearings were the moors and below were the still-wooded steep valley sides. But soil was poor and farming was limited to growing mainly oats and keeping a few animals, including some cows, maybe some sheep and perhaps a horse or a donkey for transport purposes. Scraping a living was hard and people were forced to think of ways to earn more money.[2]

1. Sheep gave the weavers their raw material.

They combined farming their small plots of land with producing woollen cloth. By the fifteenth century cottagers who could afford to buy a handloom were making woollen cloth for their household needs and making extra cloth to sell at market. Producing cloth was a family affair with the children carding the wool, the wives spinning it and the men weaving. Carding, straightening wool fibres, was done using pairs of hand cards made of bent iron pins set in leather and mounted on wood.[3] Spinning was done using a wheel. After the cloth had been woven it was fulled and finished and then the cottager would take it to the local market. He would either carry the cloth on his back or if he had one his donkey would carry it for him. He returned home with any profit and a new supply of wool so the family could produce more cloth. In time the more successful cottagers became the clothiers who had established themselves at the top of production units. They bought wool and employed cottagers to card, spin and weave it into the cloth which they then collected and marketed. In 1588 there was plenty of work for carders and spinners because it took twenty carders and spinners to keep four weavers busy.[4]

For centuries woollen cloth production had been widespread in England but in the Calder Valley, then a remote area, conditions were not ideal. Wool had to be brought in from other areas because the local sheep produced wool which was too coarse to make good quality cloth.[5] Also transporting goods to and from markets was difficult. As trade increased, trains of packhorses had to be used because the causeways over the hills were narrow and steep, making them unsuitable for horse-drawn carts. Textiles became successful in the Calder Valley because of the ambition of the clothiers and the local geography. High rainfall produced fast flowing streams which tumbled down tributary valleys to feed the River Calder, giving the area power which could be used to turn wheels. Also the water was "soft water", which gives a good lather with soap, for, amongst other things, washing dirt and grease out of raw wool.

Fulling Mills

Woollen cloth from the loom had to be fulled, that is, scoured, cleaned and thickened by beating it in soapy water so that the short fibres of wool would mat together to give the cloth strength. As far back as the Middle Ages this process had been mechanised, and using power from a waterwheel, large wooden hammers, fulling stocks, were worked noisily up and down to pound cloth. Cottagers took their pieces of cloth to the local fulling mill to be "milled" and then they took them home to hang them on tenter frames where they were stretched and dried in the open air. Finishing the cloth involved raising its nap using dried teasels mounted on handles and then the rough nap was neatly cropped with cropping shears.

The Lud flows down past Luddenden to meet the River Calder at the place which came to be known as Luddenden Foot and in 1588, at the foot of the Lud, using power from waterwheels, there were two small fulling mills. The Weavers Arms pub stands on the footprint of the mill which was run by Henry Farrar and on the other side of the Lud stood the mill run by Michael Foxcroft. A housing development now stands on the footprint of Foxcroft's mill. In 1599 there was "trouble at mill" when these two men had an argument about water rights and their dispute grew until it resulted in "two murders and several affrays".[6] Foxcroft destroyed Farrar's dam and so Farrar destroyed Foxcroft's dam which was further upstream. The royal cartographer to Elizabeth I, Christopher Saxton, was sent to draw maps of the stream, the dams and the watercourses and the case was heard in the Duchy Court.[7] Foxcroft was ordered to pay for the damage but in his defence he said that when Farrar and his friends retaliated they "had come weaponed with swords, daggers and rapiers, long piked staves, pitch forks, iron forks, gavelocks and picks" and they'd destroyed his dam and blocked his goit (water course). He said that Farrar "had kept an armed guard on the spot for three weeks".

There have been two other fulling mills in the area but they were on the River Calder which at the time was a clean, clear river. In 1599 Boy Mill was on the Sowerby side of the Calder.[8] In 1738 Longbottom Mill was working on the Warley side of the Calder near Daisy Bank.[9]

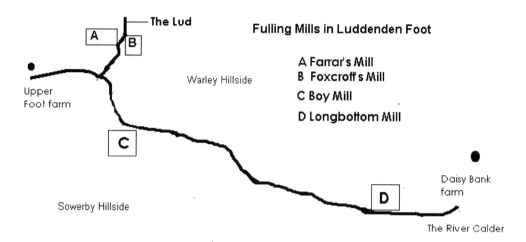

Henry Briggs the mathematician

Before the disturbances at the Luddenden Foot fulling mills, in 1561, a baby boy was born at Daisy Bank Farm. He was called Henry Briggs and he spent his childhood in the area but his adult life was to be spent not in subsistence farming and weaving cloth but in the country's great centres of learning. By 1577 Briggs, then sixteen years old, was studying at St John's College Cambridge where in 1585 he got his master's degree. In 1596 he went on to become Professor of Geometry at Gresham College, London where he stayed for over twenty years. It was at Gresham College that Briggs met Lord Napier who in 1614 had published his work on logarithms. Briggs developed an easier way to use Napier's logarithms and he spent his life producing the Briggian Logarithm tables which are still used today. In 1620 he became the first Savilian Professor of Geometry at Merton College Oxford where he was considered to be "the most learned man of his time in geometrical matters". He died in 1631 and was buried at Merton College, Oxford, many miles from his humble beginnings at Daisy Bank Farm in the Luddenden Foot area of the Calder Valley.[10]

Kershaw House

In the seventeenth century yeomen clothiers were landowners who had made their money from cloth production and they built many of the grand houses that are still standing on the hillsides around Calderdale. One of the wealthiest of these clothiers was James Murgatroyd who was born at The Hollins in Warley. He built many houses including Kershaw House which is in Luddenden Lane, just above Luddenden Foot.

Worsteds

Worsteds, finer cloths than woollens, were being woven in East Anglia and the West of England. In the production of woollens, wool is carded into short fibres which are spun into a thick yarn which produces coarse cloth that needs to be fulled. But in the production of worsteds, the wool is combed into long fibres and the yarn produced by the spinners is stronger and finer. Worsted cloth does not need to be fulled and the warp and weft of the weave is still seen in the finished cloth which is generally lighter and smoother than woollen cloth. At the beginning of the eighteenth century there were clothiers in the Calder Valley who wanted the worsted trade and Samuel Hill of Making Place in Soyland was amongst those who introduced worsteds to this area. By 1800 the West Riding was producing sixty per cent of the nation's output and its wool and worsted trade meant that the West Riding of Yorkshire would become, for a time, one of the greatest cloth-producing areas in the world.[11] [12]

By the 1760s a weaver no longer threw the shuttle across his loom by hand. Kay's Flying Shuttle, originally invented for cotton, had been adapted for wool and the weaver could now move his shuttle by pulling on cords. It meant that he could weave cloth that was wider than he could stretch his arms and it also allowed him to work faster which meant he needed to be supplied with yarn at an even faster rate. This problem was partly solved by the invention of the Spinning Jenny which could spin forty threads of yarn at a time. Cloth was still made by hand in the cottages but production was faster, more cloth was sold and clothiers prospered.[13]

The turnpike road

By the mid-eighteenth century the cloth trade was thriving and with increasing trade there was a need for a better road which would be suitable for horse-drawn carts carrying heavy loads of cloth, wool and cotton to and from markets. Privately financed turnpike trusts were set up and by the 1770s a road had been built from Halifax to Todmorden through the valley bottom. The road was wide with gentle gradients and became the main highway connecting the Calder Valley with the wool and worsted industries of the West Riding and with Lancashire's cotton industry. So that investors could recover their money, there was a charge for travelling along the road and at intervals there were toll houses with bars across the road which would be raised when payment had been made. There was a toll bar at Friendly and another at the entrance to

Daisy Bank, an area which is still known as Bar Wood. This one was removed in 1858 and placed in the village centre at Danny Lane just below the White House, which at the time was occupied by the village blacksmith. There was also a toll bar at Naylor Lane just above the present Burnley Road Council School, and the farmer, John Naylor of Little Longbottom, collected the tolls.[14]

The Rochdale Canal

By 1798 another highway passed through Luddenden Foot. Canals were being built to assist trade because water carriage was cheaper than transport on land. The Rochdale Canal between Sowerby Bridge and Manchester was built as part of the system which crossed the country linking Hull with Liverpool. The stretch between Sowerby Bridge and Todmorden was opened on the 24th August 1798 and the link to Manchester was completed by 1804. It took navvies only eight years, using picks and shovels, to build the Rochdale Canal which crossed the Pennines and contained the largest number of locks per mile of any canal in England. Because of the climb, canal builders needed to take water to work locks from the River Calder and its tributaries. But manufacturers were jealous of their water supply which they needed for their corn, fulling, carding and spinning mills. Disputes about water rights eased when compromises were reached and reservoirs were created to manage the supply of water to the canal system.[15]

2. The aqueduct carrying the Rochdale Canal over the Lud. 2010
At Luddenden Foot when the canal was cut, a small aqueduct was needed. The Lud flows under
the road and then under the canal before it joins the River Calder.

Barges were loaded and unloaded in the village at the canal basin which was on the Park side of the bridge over the canal. Horses working in relays were used to pull canal barges, which carried loads of lime and manure, stone, slate, coal, machinery, corn,[16] flour, cotton, raw wool, and finished cloth. Often barges carried many tons of cargo and "one horse dragging a barge on a canal could pull as much weight as six hundred packhorses could carry."[17] The heavy loads of coal that barges carried became essential when water-powered mills were converted to steam power because although there were local outcrops, the supply was small and in the steam-driven textile factories, huge amounts of coal were needed.[18]

Early textile mills

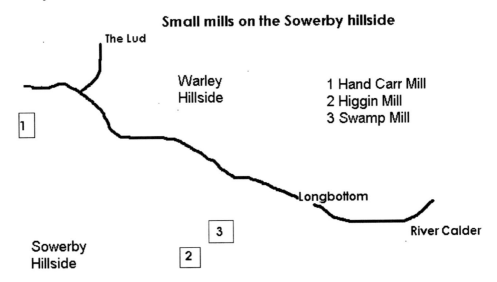

In 1758[19] Hand Carr or Clough Mill was water-powered and situated in a narrow valley above the site which in the 1840s would house the village railway station. In the early 1800s it was a worsted spinning mill.[20]

In the mid-1800s there was a worsted mill at Higgin Chamber and Greenwood wrote about this mill that, "On Friday evening, September 5th 1856, it was burnt down but never rebuilt and on the place where it stood there subsequently were built a number of cottages out of the ruins of the old mill."[21]

There was also a small woollen mill at Swamp.[22]

Around 1800, Upper Foot Farm was one of the few houses at Luddenden Foot and it was the home of William Currer who was an Overseer of the Poor[23] in the township of Midgley and a well-known local manufacturer. He ran Foxcroft's old mill, now known as Luddenden Foot Mill, and he also ran Boy Mill. The River Calder was spanned by a narrow stone bridge which had been paid for by William Currer and the township of Sowerby. It was known as the Currer Bridge and it allowed the manufacturer to have access to Boy Mill. It was the only bridge over the Calder between Brierley and Longbottom Mill. [24]

Methods of cloth production were changing and the inventiveness of the industry made it possible for manufacturers to increase profits by producing more cloth more cheaply. Hand-held cards had been replaced by carding machines and these machines could also be used for scribbling, which was the mixing together of different colours of dyed wool in preparation for spinning. Spinning was another process no longer done by hand. Old fulling mills were being enlarged and adapted to house new machinery and manufacturers were running a number of processes under one roof. At Luddenden Foot Mill, William Currer had scribbling, carding and slubbing machines which prepared wool for spinning, a handloom weaving shop, a large carpet weaving shop, and fulling stocks.[25] It was William Currer who taught John Crossley how to make carpets.[26] Currer also had cotton-spinning machines and in February 1805 he presided over a meeting of Halifax manufacturers, when it was decided to allow for the first time the sale of cotton goods in the Halifax Piece Hall.[27]

3. The small round house at Tenterfields. Stansfield Hall is at the top on the right. Beulah Place is on the left. Parts of the walls of the house were still there in the 1960s.

In 1782 the old fulling mill at Longbottom was enlarged into a four-storey establishment which housed a hand-weaving shop, two drying houses, and two warehouses.[28] In the fields around the mill there were wooden tenter frames with tenter hooks on which the woollen cloth, after it had been fulled, was stretched to the correct width and hung out to dry. The area below Burnley Road, just above what was Longbottom Mill, is still called Tenter Fields and at the top of the field there is the footprint of a small round house. It is said that it was the home of a man whose job it was to bring in the cloth from the tenterframes if it started to rain."[29]

The early 1800s were difficult times for textile workers. From 1792 to 1815 when Britain was at war with Napoleon's France the worsted industry had difficulty exporting cloth because, in an attempt to starve Britain, the French were blockading European ports. Because of falling trade there were bankruptcies and unemployment and, making things worse, there were bad harvests resulting in high prices for corn. After the wars were over, trade remained depressed and many textile workers went hungry.

These hard times were described by Dorothy Wordsworth, sister of the poet, who visited friends in the Halifax area in 1817. In one of her letters home she wrote:

"The country here is varied and beautiful, if it were not for the cotton and woollen mills, which are really now no more than encumbrances, trade being so bad. The wealthy keep their mills going chiefly for the value of employing workmen. Few get more than half work, great numbers none at all. A great part of the population is reduced to pauperism, a dreadful evil."[30]

Raising the nap on woollen cloth, once done with hand-held dried teasels,[31] was increasingly being done by machines in gig mills. At this time another of the textile finishing processes, cropping, had been mechanised. Croppers were highly skilled men who trimmed the rough nap on cloth using cropping shears. But because a cropping frame tended by one man could do the work of ten hand-croppers, manufacturers were installing them in their gig mills in the hope of cheapening their products and avoiding bankruptcy.[32] The hand croppers were facing unemployment and they violently resisted the mechanisation of their jobs. Many districts in the West Riding of Yorkshire had groups of men who armed themselves, smashed cropping machines, and threatened the manufacturers who installed them. In 1812 these men, Luddites,[33] hard to track down because they had sworn oaths of loyalty and secrecy, were active in the Huddersfield and Halifax areas in the Colne Valley, the Spen Valley and the Calder Valley.

When the military finally smashed the Luddites in 1813, sixty-four men were held and put on trial at York and of these men, fifteen were resident in the parish of Halifax at the time of their alleged Luddite activities. Seventeen men were hanged and six of these were from the Halifax parish. Three of them were found guilty of burglary and three were found guilty of breaking cropping frames. One of them was William Hartley from Warley who was a widower and a father of eight. He was hanged for machine-breaking and stealing arms from the farm of George Haigh at Copley Gate in Skircoat. Another, Joseph Crowther who was a Sowerby cotton-spinner, was hanged for stealing arms. Eleven men were transported and of these five were from the Halifax parish. They were found guilty of administering illegal oaths.[34]

8

By 1817 in Yorkshire cloth-finishing there were 72 gig mills and 1,462 cropping machines. Of the croppers 1,170 had no work, 1,445 were working part-time and only 763 were working full-time.[35]

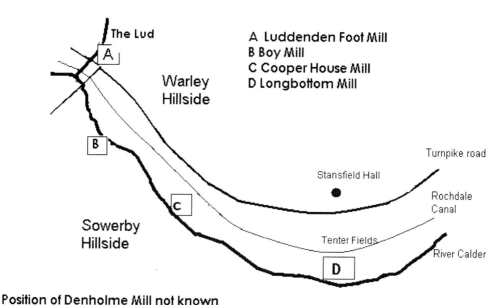

A Luddenden Foot Mill
B Boy Mill
C Cooper House Mill
D Longbottom Mill

The Lud

Warley Hillside

Turnpike road

Stansfield Hall

Rochdale Canal

Sowerby Hillside

Tenter Fields

River Calder

Position of Denholme Mill not known

Mills in Luddenden Foot 1800-1830

After the Napoleonic Wars when the economy recovered there was money to be made by enterprising people, and in the main it was the wealthy clothiers and their families who could raise the capital to invest in mills and machinery. Sometimes there were half-way stages between the domestic system and the factory system of cloth production where, for example, weavers would work together in one place but they were not operating machines: they were still handloom weaving. This happened at Boy Mill, the old fulling mill at Luddenden Foot, which had previously been run as a cotton mill by Messrs. Briggs who lived at Bottoms. It was occupied in 1829 by the Ackroyds and they ran it as a worsted mill. Because Luddenden handloom weavers were considered to be "amongst the best in the area", they brought them down from the Luddenden valley to work together in the mill weaving "stout goods made from two fold warps". In 1847-48, when their lease ran out the Ackroyds moved to Copley and at some time after that the Whitworths moved into Boy Mill. [36] [37]

By the 1830s working life for handloom weavers hadn't significantly changed. They were mainly still working in the relative freedom of their cottages on the hillsides.

Woolcombers, who combed wool for the worsted spinners, also worked at home. Their combing room was often the bedroom and because the metal combs they used had to be hot there was always a fire and sometimes a number of men would work together to save money on fuel. The hot combs were fixed to a pole in the centre of the room and wool was dragged through them until it was in soft, straight fibres. Long fibres of wool would be sent down to the worsted spinning mills in the valley and any short fibres would be sent to woollen workers.[38]

Child Labour

By the 1830s for children and young women there had been dramatic changes in lifestyle. Their jobs had been mechanised. Now, instead of working at home carding and spinning by hand, they had to work in factories and tend machines and on the whole they were thoroughly exploited by the manufacturers.

"We know that fathers took their children out of bed before five o'clock on a dark winter's morning, and carried them on their shoulders to the mill. Clocks were a luxury, and many children, afraid of being late, were at the mill gates long before the opening hour, and the tired little mites would fall asleep until wakened by the rattle of machinery."[39]

Cooper House Mill, on the Warley side of the Calder, was built in 1832. It was run by Samuel and William Smith and they also ran Denholme Mill which was between Boy Mill and Cooper House Mill. They were worsted spinners. At their mills in Luddenden Foot they employed 125 people, only seven of whom (5.6 per cent) were over 21 years old, and "they were working from 6am until 8pm but stopped early on Saturday at 5 o'clock. There was also a night shift which worked from 8pm until 6am."[40] The local newspaper reported that there was a fire at Smiths' worsted mill on the night of 28th November 1832. It was caused by a boy employee who lit his lantern with a spindle band which he then threw away before it was quenched. Samuel Smith discovered the fire before too much damage had been done and smothered it with wool sheets and wrappers. The Smiths were working their young people through the night but the newspaper reporter's only judgement was that working a mill at night was a better safeguard than having night watchmen because "they are not always found true to their post".[41]

Textile mills in Luddenden Foot have suffered many fires. A small incident was often hard to contain because mill floors were soaked in the oil which was used to lubricate the machinery.

In the early years of the factory system there was little protection for employees. Greenwood, writing about the mills in Luddenden Foot, recalled that in 1834 " ... girls of seven years of age worked those very long, weary hours for 2s 6d a week."[42] Because operating machines was unskilled work, many jobs could be done by children. Mill owners didn't need to pay adult wages and parents needed the money their children could earn. Greenwood recalled "in connection with one mill the master used to go to homes where the children were likely to work and suggest to the parents that they should send their children to work at his mill." The children worked as pieceners and doffers under the supervision of overlookers. As pieceners they fed wool into the slubbing, scribbling and carding machines.[43] As doffers they were small enough to crawl under spinning machines to fasten loose ends of broken yarn and they also took off the bobbins which were full of yarn and replaced them with empty ones. Spinners were sometimes paid according to how much yarn was produced and so mistakes made by their child labourers would not always have been well received.

Richard Oastler, the son of a Leeds manufacturer, was a supporter of William Wilberforce, who campaigned against slavery in the West Indies. In 1830 Oastler compared the lot of children in the textile mills to the lot of African slaves in America saying "... Poor infants! Ye are indeed sacrificed at the shrine of avarice, without even the solace of the negro slaves; ... ye are no more than he is, free agents, ye are compelled to work as long as the necessity of your needy parents may require or the cold blooded avarice of your worse than barbarian masters may demand."[44]

There was much concern about the plight of children in factories and in 1831 Michael Saddler, MP for Newark, introduced The Ten Hour Bill to Parliament. He wanted:

A ten-hour day for all factory operatives who were under the age of 18 with 8 hours on Saturday all inclusive of mealtimes.

No night work for any worker under 21.

No child under the age of 9 to be allowed to work in a factory.

In 1833 when George Crabtree, a textile operative from Huddersfield, passed through the Calder Valley collecting evidence to support the Ten Hour Bill, his comment on the fine houses being built by mill owners was: "When they cannot even afford to give their workpeople wages sufficient to keep body and soul together, we passed many of them whose tattered clothes their poverty bespoke ..."

Often children were very cruelly treated. One of the interviews Crabtree conducted was with the Rev. John Crossley of St John's Church, Cragg Vale which is in the next valley to the Luddenden Foot area.

"He had interred a poor boy that used frequently to work 15 and 16 hours a day. He was aged eleven and, when he died, a short time before that he went for some (cotton) wool and he was so overcome with sleep that, when he had got his arms full of (cotton) wool, he fell down asleep with the remainder. He was missing and sought after and he was found in the posture of almost standing on his head with his arms full of (cotton) wool. The master gave him a savage beating with a strap to awaken him the poor little fellow."[45]

In 1842 the local newspaper in an article on "White Slavery in England"[46] reported that "factory children are subject to many accidents on account of the dangerous state of the machinery, from the want of proper boxing off, and many lives are lost yearly by the neglect of this precaution and want of care on the part of the children."

Men like Richard Oastler, George Crabtree, and John Fielden, a Todmorden manufacturer and a Member of Parliament,[47] worked to have the Ten Hour Bill made law. Over the years there were some improvements in the working conditions of women and children but it was 1847 before the Ten Hour Bill finally passed into law.[48]

---

[1] Bernard Jennings & Hebden Bridge WEA, *Pennine Valley: a history of Upper Calderdale* (Smith Settle, 1992), 29.

[2] Jennings, *Pennine Valley*, 5.

[3] Phyllis Bentley, *The Pennine Weaver* (Cedric Chivers Ltd 1970), 28.

[4] Bentley, *The Pennine Weaver*, 29.

[5] Jennings, *Pennine Valley*, 80.

[6] G R Binns, "Water Wheels in the Upper Calder Valley," *Trans. Halifax Antiq. Soc.* (1972).

[7] Jennings *Pennine Valley*, 46, Saxton's map.

[8] Binns, "Water Wheels in the Upper Calder Valley," *Trans. Halifax Antiq. Soc.* (1972).

[9] Binns, "Water Wheels in the Upper Calder Valley," *Trans. Halifax Antiq. Soc.* (1972).

[10] T W Hanson *The Story of Old Halifax*, 109.
D M Hallowes,"Henry Briggs .Mathematician," *Trans. Halifax Antiq. Soc.* (Nov. 1961).

[11] Hanson, *The Story of Old Halifax*, 179.

[12] H Holroyde, 'Textile Mills, Masters and Men in Halifax District, 1770-1851,' *Trans. Halifax Antiq. Soc.* (April 1979).

[13] Bentley, *The Pennine Weaver*, 39, 40.

[14] J Greenwood, *Jubilee of the Luddenden Foot Industrial Co-operative Society Ltd 1860 –1910*, 20.

[15] *The Rochdale Canal* (Waterways Handbook Co., Unsworth).

[16] Any type of grain.

[17] Bentley, *The Pennine Weaver*, 32.

[18] Holroyde, "Textile Mills … Halifax 1770-1851", *Trans Halifax Antiq. Soc.* (April 1979).

[19] Binns, "Water Wheels in the Upper Calder Valley," *Trans. Halifax Antiq. Soc.* (1972).

[20] Greenwood, 16.

[21] Greenwood, 16.

[22] Greenwood, 16.

[23] Overseers of the Poor overlooked the collecting of the poor rates and the giving out of relief.

[24] Arthur Comfort, "Our Home and Country", *Halifax Courier*, 8 August 1914.

[25] Jennings, *Pennine Valley*, 110.

[26] "Today's Picture", *Halifax Evening Courier*, 25 May 1956.

[27] Built in 1779. So called because it was where the clothiers and weavers sold their pieces of cloth.

[28] Holroyde, "Textile Mills … Halifax 1770-1851", *Trans Halifax Antiq. Soc.* (April 1979).

[29] John Hargreaves, *Sowerby Bridge in Old Photographs* (Smith Settle, 1994), 190.

[30] E Webster, *Textiles and Tools: 19th Century Industries in Calderdale* (Eric Webster, 1990), 12.

[31] Plant with large prickly head.

[32] Bentley, *The Pennine Weaver*, 45.

[33] The name "Luddite" has no connection with Luddenden or Luddenden Foot.

[34] John Hargreaves, "Halifax and the Yorkshire Luddite Disturbances of 1812", *Trans. Halifax Antiq. Soc.*, (1986).

[35] James Berry, *The Luddites in Yorkshire* (Dalesman Publishing, 1970), 28.

[36] E Webster, *Textiles and Tools: 19th Century Industries in Calderdale* (Eric Webster, 1990), 12.

[37] Greenwood, 15.

[38] Angus Bethune Reach, ed. Aspin, *Fabrics, Filth and Fairy Tents* (Royd Press, 2007), 44.

[39] Hanson, *The Story of Old Halifax*, 42.

[40] Binns, "Water Wheels in the Upper Calder Valley," *Trans. Halifax Antiq. Soc.* (1972).

[41] *Halifax Guardian*, Saturday 1 December 1832.

[42] Greenwood, 17.

[43] Bentley, *The Pennine Weaver*, 55.

[44] C Spencer, "Child labour in the early textile mills" *Trans. Halifax Antiq. Soc.* 1991.

[45] Holroyde, "Textile Mills ... Halifax 1770-1851", *Trans Halifax Antiq. Soc.* (April 1979).

[46] *Halifax Guardian*, Saturday 11 June 1842.

[47] Linda Croft, *John Fielden's Todmorden* (Tygerfoot Press, 1994).

[48] C Spencer, "Child labour in the early textile mills" *Trans. Halifax Antiq. Soc.* 1991.

Chapter 2
Poverty, Petitions and Rioting

The 1840s

In 1841 in the Luddenden Foot area, 80 per cent of the working population worked in textiles. Of the men who worked, 75 per cent were in textiles, and of the women who worked outside the home, 96 per cent were in textiles. Most said they were working with woollens and worsteds but a few said they worked with cotton.[1]

Combing wool for worsted spinners was very labour-intensive because wool combing had not yet been mechanised. It occupied 19 per cent of the textile workforce and it was mainly a male occupation.

Not everyone made clear whether they worked with wool or worsteds but 269 people did say they were involved with worsted spinning[2] and they would have worked in the mills in the valley. The oldest group of these mill workers were the overlookers with an average age of 35 years and they were all men. Of the 269 people who said they worked in the worsted spinning mills, 40 per cent were male and 60 per cent were female. They were very young. The average age of male employees was 14.7 years and that of female employees was 15.1 years. Since the 1833 Factories Act no child under the age of 9 years should have been working in a mill but there were one or two in the group who were only 8 or 7 years old.

The Gardiner family lived in a cottage at Boulder Clough on the Sowerby hillside. John and his wife, Hannah, both 35 years old, were wool combers; their oldest son William, who was 17 years old, was a weaver, Robert, 15 years old, was a wool comber, John, 12 years, and Richard, 7 years, both worked in a worsted factory, and then there were Rebecca and Sarah who were only 5 years old and one year old. When poor people wanted to go anywhere they had to walk and many, like young John and Richard Gardiner, after spending a long day in the mill, would have faced the climb back up the hillside to their homes. If they were lucky they would be wearing the footwear that the poor people wore: clogs. When it was dark they may have carried lighted candles in jars to help them on their way.[3]

In 1841 in the Luddenden Foot area, on the Sowerby and Warley hillsides, there were eighteen small farms. Upper Longbottom farm was on the Warley hillside and its occupant was "independent" and described himself as "Squire Murgatroyd".[4] At the other end of the social scale many farmers were supplementing their incomes by wool combing, weaving or by having their children work in the spinning mills.

The village corn mill

In 1841 Luddenden Foot Mill had two occupiers who were sharing the power from the Lud. Samuel Turner was in woollens and William Thompson ran a corn mill. Thompson, who was 55 years old and living at Middle Foot, described himself as a corn dealer and maltster. Also working at the mill was his son George who was 30 years old and another member of the family, William H. Thompson, who was 24 years old. [5]

Greenwood wrote that the Thompsons "were for a long time a very prosperous firm and 'Thompson's Flour' was a household word; it was known not only in the village but very widely throughout the country."[6] Corn would be bought in local markets such as Halifax and taken by the sackful to the mill when flour was needed.[7]

In 1841 nearly 2,000 people lived in the Luddenden Foot area and 570 people lived in the village.[8] Workers needed to live within walking distance of their work and as the village grew, houses were built in the spaces that were available. In Luddenden Foot this meant building in the narrow valley along the roadside and in spaces which were often very close to mills. Housing in the village at this time was at "Luddenden Foot", Denholme, Boys Scarr, Ellen Holme, Cooper House Mill Cottages, Brick Houses and Railway Cottage. There were 92 small houses, with an average of 6 people per house and so there was a good deal of overcrowding.

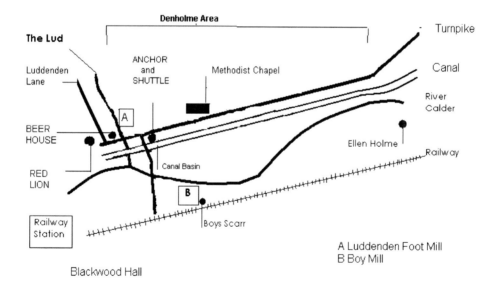

Luddenden Foot village in 1841

There were sandstone quarries above Middle Foot and Upper Foot,[9] and in Luddenden Foot men worked in the construction business as: excavators, stone masons, builders, slate layers, plasterers, joiners and painters.

In the road haulage business there were carters, a cart builder, a horse dealer and blacksmiths. There were watermen whose work would have been on the canal and there were three railway workers.

The railway

Until the 1840s horses provided the power for transport by pulling coaches, carts and barges through the valley. Now the world was changing. The power of steam had been harnessed to pull loads along tracks and this brought the third highway through Luddenden Foot, the Manchester and Leeds Railway. Luddenden Foot Railway Station was opened in October 1840 and from there firms like Boy Mill and Cooper House Mill could dispatch their products. [10] Coal for domestic heating and industrial power was delivered to the sidings to be collected and delivered to customers.

Greenwood wrote of when the railway was being built saying, "the old sleepy, monotonous days were gradually passing away. The few inhabitants of the Dale were greatly interested in watching the army of navvies ... cutting, carving, and boring through every obstacle to their progress." He went on to say that the railway was "an object of very great curiosity, the people travelled from great distances to see the trains." The coming of the railway meant that for the first time poor people could travel well beyond their immediate surroundings and Greenwood said: "When the line was extended to Hull an excursion was run there from this district and many availed themselves of the opportunity of seeing a seaport town." But, he added, coaches then were not covered and passengers travelled standing up.[11]

Branwell Bronte

Amongst those excited by the coming of the railway was Branwell Bronte who lived at the parsonage in Haworth with his evangelical father, his aunt and his three talented sisters, Charlotte, Emily and Anne. In 1839, when he was twenty-two, Branwell would travel the few miles over the moors from Haworth to Hebden Bridge or Todmorden to watch the railway being built. He also visited Luddenden Foot because he was drawn to the colourful canal barges and the boatmen who worked on them. Stores and equipment needed to build the railway were brought up the valley by barge and the boatmen would tie up for the night in the canal basin at Luddenden Foot. They would drink in the Anchor and Shuttle, in front of the canal basin, the Red Lion Inn, at the bottom of Luddenden Lane[12] or the beer house next to the corn mill.[13] Tough and crude, boatmen led carefree lives travelling the waterways and they were very different from the poets, sculptors and painters who until then had been Branwell's usual companions.

In 1840, after failing to have his poetry published, with little success as a portrait painter and having decided that teaching was not for him, Branwell dismayed his family by taking a job as a booking clerk at Sowerby Bridge Railway Station. He kept in touch with old friends like the poet William Dearden who lived in Sowerby Bridge, and who in 1847 would become head master of Warley Grammar School, but his new friends included railwaymen and boatmen. He drank with them at the Navigation pub near the canal in Sowerby Bridge. Branwell had been a member of the Haworth Temperance Society but now he was drinking and taking laudanum.

4. There is a small statue of Branwell Bronte at the entrance to the site which used to house Luddenden Foot's railway station. 2010

In April 1841, after six months at Sowerby Bridge, he was transferred to Luddenden Foot Station where his title was Station Master. But after Sowerby Bridge, a busy junction, a job on the quiet branchline at Luddenden Foot was not much of a promotion. He became a regular at the Lord Nelson at Luddenden where the Luddenden Reading Society held its meetings and where he met John Whitworth. John was a more sober man and someone who would make a huge contribution to the development of Luddenden Foot. Branwell's other friends were down in Luddenden Foot near the canal at the Anchor and

Shuttle and the Red Lion. There he drank with boatmen and the village's Liverpool Irish, a group of people who were disliked by the locals because they "sold their labour cheap". He also spent time with George and William H. Thompson from the village corn mill.

Branwell's lifestyle took its toll and in January 1842 he lost his job because he'd been negligent and the station accounts were badly kept. After working only fifteen months on the railways he returned home to the parsonage to report his disgrace and another humiliating failure. A tragic figure, overshadowed by the success of his sisters, he died in September 1848 when he was only thirty-one years old. [14]

The Methodists

5. The Burnley Road entrance to the footprint of the Methodist chapel in Luddenden Foot. 2010

Across the road and a little way up from the present Post Office on Burnley Road is the footprint of the demolished Lower Denholme Methodist Chapel. The rusty chapel railings are still on the wall above the pavement and steps beyond the gate lead to an abandoned graveyard. In 1841 this was the only place of worship in the village and it had been there since 1832.[15]

Apart from a small immigrant Irish community who belonged to the Catholic Church, those who were religious in the Calder Valley were mainly nonconformists who believed that the church should be separate from the state. Methodists, so called because of their methodical ways,[16] liked to organise their own affairs and worship in their own way. They already had chapels in the townships on the hillsides and now because the valleys were becoming more populated, they were building chapels there too. Many mill owners were non-conformists and they preached sobriety, hard work, thrift and self improvement.[17]

The founder members of the Methodist Chapel in Luddenden Foot included at least five of the village mill owners.[18] There was the corn miller, William Thompson and his son George who eight years later would be one of Branwell Bronte's friends. Two others were Samuel and William Smith who were running night shifts at Cooper House and Denholme Mills. Thomas Ackroyd who ran Boy Mill, James and William Haigh, Paul Greenwood, John Horsefield, Thomas Spencer and Robert Thorp were the other trustees and this was their statement at their first meeting on May 30th 1832:

"The friends of humanity and religion have thought it advisable for the good of the inhabitants and the rising generation in and around Luddenden Foot to erect a small preaching house or school room for their accommodation. We therefore whose names are here inscribed come forward as trustees for the said place intended to be erected on a plot of ground belonging to the Emmotts Estate situated at Luddenden Foot and taken by us on conditions as will be afterwards stated."

At first the chapel was to be modest but it developed into an imposing presence. It was a square building with three windows on each side and with two in the end which overlooked the turnpike road. There were also two circular windows high on the end wall and a double door entrance. Inside there was to be a gallery and one of the trustees, John Horsefield, was engaged to build it for £52 under the following condition: "the said work was to be finished by 16th March and for every day before that he was to receive 1d and for every day after that he was to pay 1d." Methodists needed no lessons in project management.

In Victorian England it was common practice to pay money to reserve a pew in church and the more you paid the better your seat; and this was a statement about your status in the community. In September 1874 at the Methodists' chapel there was a pew-holders' meeting to discuss alterations in recommended prices. Seats which were on each side and in front of the preacher's platform were to be 1/- per quarter, all sittings behind the preacher were to be 9d per quarter. The two corner pews at the end of the chapel nearest to the road were to be 1/4d per sitting and the two back seats between the corner pews were to be 1d per sitting. Sitting in the two long pews at the back of the chapel was to be free.[19] This would raise some money for the chapel but it also meant that the poorest were left in no doubt about where they belonged.

In the 1840s those of Luddenden Foot's labouring poor who chose the fellowship of the chapel over the fellowship of the village pubs did so on the only day of the week that they were not required at work. The chapel, whose founder members included a number of local employers, was concerned with their members' Christian morality, with their intellectual improvement and with their sobriety. But survival was the main concern of the poor. They lived in fear of illness, fear of short time at the mill, fear of no work, fear of having to ask for poor relief and fear of the workhouse.

The workhouse

In 1834 the Poor Law Amendment Act had come into force. Poor relief in the agricultural areas in the south was becoming too expensive for parish ratepayers to bear and the government was determined to stop "any form of relief to the able-bodied which might lessen the will to work". Responsibility for helping the poor was taken away from the townships, which were then grouped into Unions with elected Boards of Guardians. Sowerby, Warley and Midgley, the townships which governed the Luddenden Foot area, became part of the Halifax Poor Law Union and in 1841 the Halifax Union Workhouse opened. Previously, poor relief had been given to people in their homes as "out-relief", and this had worked well because in industrial areas when trade was depressed, mills didn't always close: instead, the workers would work part-time or accept reduced wages. With the new system, there was to be no more "out-relief" for the able-bodied. They either got no relief or they went into the workhouse. In trade downturns, more people than could be catered for in the workhouse needed help and so Halifax continued to provide some "out-relief". In the workhouse food was very similar to the food which the poorest workers usually ate, which was mainly oatmeal, potatoes, and milk, with some occasional bacon. It was the deliberately harsh regime, which often included the separation of men, wives and children that really frightened people.[20]

Education

Methodists believed in self-improvement and education, and when the state did nothing and when many of the ruling classes were warning against it, they were teaching children to read and write. Before 1832 there had been a Sunday school assembly in Boy Mill which at the time was run by the Ackroyds. After 1832 the Methodists ran afternoon school for the "poorly clad and poorly fed" village children in the basement of their new chapel. One consequence, however, of teaching the working classes to read, which was feared by the ruling classes, was that the poor wouldn't limit their reading to the scriptures. There was other literature out there and some of it was written by the Chartists.

The Chartists

Chartists wanted more democracy and a fair share of the enormous wealth that badly paid workers were helping to create for the country.

They had a "People's Charter" with six demands which were for:
universal male suffrage, vote by secret ballot, annual Parliaments, equal electoral districts, payment of members of Parliament and the abolition of property qualifications for MPs.

One July day in 1842 the Chartist leader, Feargus O'Connor, who was touring Lancashire and Yorkshire, got off the train at Luddenden Foot station.[21] He was met there by about 20,000 people and together they set off in procession to Hebden Bridge and Todmorden. Chartists publicised their cause by holding processions to mass rallies and they often carried banners and were accompanied by brass bands.[22] Two months earlier the Chartists had presented their second national petition, containing over three million signatures,[23] to Parliament, but it had been rejected just as their first petition had been rejected in 1839. There had been much anger amongst activists and the government had feared a national uprising. There is evidence that around 1840 Chartists in Midgley were preparing for armed revolt: [24]

"Midgley men made weapons for themselves out of bars of iron, scythes and the like, and it was related to me long ago that they even experimented with home-made bombs in the form of gunpowder in bottles which they exploded by way of experiment in Well Lane below Lacy Hey."

England's poor were in despair. They suffered trade depressions, lowered wages and increased food prices. Harvests had been poor and a heavy duty had to be paid on any imported corn which kept the price of bread high. Many workers were starving: "clemmed to death". In the 1840s Elizabeth Gaskell wrote about the textile workers she knew:[25]

"I had always felt a deep sympathy with the careworn men, who looked as if doomed to struggle through their lives in strange alternations between work and want; tossed to and fro by circumstances ... the bitter complaints made by them, of the neglect they experienced from the prosperous – especially from the masters whose fortunes they had helped to build up ... they seem to me to be left in a state wherein lamentations and tears are thrown aside as useless, but in which the lips are compressed for curses, and the hands clenched and ready to smite."

The Plug Riots

August 1842 brought the Great Strike which began in the Midlands, spreading to Lancashire and Yorkshire and further north into Scotland and also into Wales. In the Calder Valley this led to the Plug Riots. Workers, with Chartists' support, were striking about wage cuts. In the Calder Valley some mills were now powered by steam and thousands, many from Lancashire, marched from mill to mill pulling the plugs out of the boilers if the millworkers didn't volunteer to stop working. They also threatened to disable water-powered mills. It was estimated that about 25,000 men and women, including thousands from Bradford, eventually arrived in Halifax where they were stopped and dispersed by two companies of infantry, two troops of hussars and two or three hundred special constables.[26] [27]

Joseph Greenwood recalled seeing the plug rioters when he was a boy and wrote: "I well remember seeing the crowd after it had left Hebden Bridge ... a long black straggling line of people, who cheerfully went along, evidently possessed of an idea that they were doing something towards a betterment ... The people went along over Fallingroyd Bridge towards Hawksclough ... and on to Halifax where other contingents from Yorkshire had gathered ... The streets became blocked and it was said there were 25,000 women and men there. They were poorly clad, and many were without shoes and stockings, barefoot."

The strikers turned up Cragg Vale when they arrived at Mytholmroyd but people in Luddenden Foot must have been at least aware of the rioting going on around them.

Luddenden Foot didn't escape the hardships of the 1840s. Smiths' worsted spinners at Cooper House Mill failed and, according to Greenwood, this caused a great shortage of work in the area and many removals: "blocks of houses were left standing empty with scarcely a whole pane of glass in their window frames."[28] Faced with the workhouse, people had no choice but to move to other districts to try to find employment. Some walked to work that they'd found at Lee Mill, Halifax, which was run by the Whitworth family. Others walked to work at Copley and they had to leave home in the morning between 4am and 5am in order to arrive in time. [29]

Irish migration

Ireland's poor, especially in the west of Ireland, lived mainly off potatoes. In 1845 and in successive years because of particularly wet weather, potato blight thrived causing the potatoes to rot in the fields. That meant famine and hundreds of thousands of people died in the six years before 1851. A million starving Irish, mostly poor Catholics, had no alternative but to leave their rented plots of land and their country.[30] They went to places like America, Canada, New Zealand and some came to England and some arrived in Luddenden Foot.

---

[1] 1841 census returns.

[2] Factory hands, piecesners, doffers, spinners, drawers, twisters, winders, reelers and overlookers.

[3] Marie Hartley and Joan Ingilby, *Life and Tradition in West Yorkshire* (Dent, 1976), 44.

[4] 1841 census returns.

[5] 1841 census returns.

[6] Greenwood, 20.

[7] Jennings, *Pennine Valley*, 80.

[8] 1841 census returns.

[9] OS map 1854.

[10] Hargreaves, *Sowerby Bridge in old Photographs*.

[11] Greenwood, 13, 14, 15.

[12] The Red Lion was demolished and replaced by the General Rawdon Hotel in 1879 and is now known as The Coach and Horses. The Anchor and Shuttle was replaced in 1886 by The Victoria Hotel, still an impressive building, which now houses the Post Office.

[13] Later known as the Weaver's Arms pub.

[14] Details of Branwell Bronte's life in Sowerby Bridge and Luddenden Foot from Daphne du Maurier, *The Infernal World of Branwell Bronte* (Virago Press 2006).

[15] WYAS HB, 62.

[16] John Munsey Turner, *Thunderclaps from Heaven* (Metropolitan Borough of Calderdale 1984), 5.

[17] Jennings, *Pennine Valley*, 128.

[18] Occupations from 1841 census.

[19] West Yorkshire Archives HB, 63.

[20] Jennings, *Pennine Valley*, 146-150.

[21] Hargreaves, *Sowerby Bridge in Old Photographs*, 61.

[22] Croft, *John Fielden's Todmorden*, 60.

[23] Jennings, *Pennine Valley*, 153.

[24] Croft, *John Fielden's Todmorden*, 58. Her reference: H W Harwood, *The Midgley Story: A hundred years of Co-operation* (no publisher, undated).

[25] Elizabeth Gaskell, Preface to *Mary Barton*.

[26] Croft, *John Fielden's Todmorden*, 61- 65.

[27] Hanson, *Story of Old Halifax*, 255.

[28] Greenwood, 18.

[29] Greenwood, 17, 18.

[30] J F C Harrison, *Early Victorian Britain* 1832-51 (Fontana 1988), 19.

Chapter 3
Education, Self Help and Co-operation

The Whitworth family invests in the village

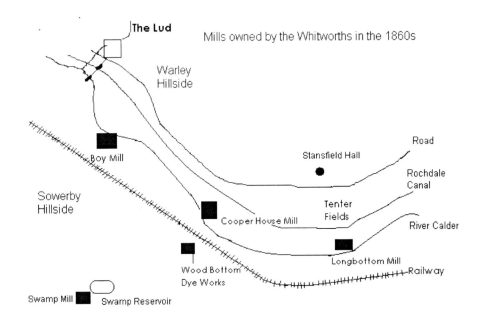

After the despair of the 1840s, in the 1850s trade picked up and at this time the Whitworth brothers, John and William, with their cousin, Robert Whitworth,[1] invested heavily in Luddenden Foot. John Whitworth was born in 1814 in Luddenden where he lived with his family at Peel House. As a young man he attended Booth Congregationalist Chapel where he was a Sunday school teacher. His family ran Peel House Mill until about 1832 when they moved to Halifax.[2] The future of Luddenden Foot was greatly influenced by the Whitworth family who by 1864 would be providing most of the employment in the area, building houses, providing another chapel with a school and supplying gas to the village.

The three Whitworths took equal shares in Cooper House Mill[3] where, in 1851, Robert Whitworth was the first worsted spinner in the Upper Calder Valley to successfully mechanise wool combing.[4] In 1862 they built a very large new mill at Cooper House, which was run as a cotton mill, and close by they established Wood Bottom Dye Works. In 1865 they built a reservoir at Swamp, near Finkle Street, to supply the dye works with water.

6. The archway which was the entrance to the mill yard at Cooper House can still be seen from the canal bank below the Congregationalist chapel. 2010.

In 1858 the Whitworths rebuilt Boy Mill as a seven-storey mill, which produced woollens. Nearby they built a number of machine shops, employing mechanics, masons, joiners and blacksmiths.[5]

By 1864 they'd also taken over Swamp Mill and the woollen mill at Longbottom, which had previously been owned by the Turner family.

The village and the Whitworth family had their share of disasters. Heavy rainfall sometimes caused catastrophic flooding in the valley, and Greenwood tells of the mill at Longbottom suffering more from floods than any other in the district. He said that, "On November 16th 1866 a great flood occurred which inundated the mill, sheds, machinery and adjacent fields, swept the wooden bridge from its position, caused much loss for the firm, and considerably inconvenienced the workpeople." There was no other way over the river from Sowerby to Warley between Sowerby Bridge and Cooper House Mill.[6]

Steam power

Most cloth was now made not in cottages but in factories, and the introduction of the power loom meant deafeningly noisy weaving sheds had been established. Machines were now driven by steam power. Waterpower had been very cheap but one disadvantage had been that in periods of drought, when there was less water to turn the wheel, work in the mill had to stop. When textiles were produced by cottagers in their homes, if the fulling mill stopped, the cottager could turn to farming, but in the factory system the mill stopping meant the manufacturer lost money.[7] Initially steam power was used to help out at times of drought by pumping water from a mill's tailrace back to the dam so it could be reused.[8] But the superiority of steam was realised when more power was needed as more processes were mechanised and mills became larger to accommodate the machinery. Steam power meant mills, dependent now on coal to heat the water in the boilers, no longer needed to be sited by streams or rivers. Now the place to be was near to the coal supply: the canal wharf or the railway sidings. Coal, the fuel of the industrial revolution, was used to power trains, to power mills, to heat homes and to produce town gas.

The lives of textile workers had been changed forever and now their surroundings, described by Dorothy Wordsworth in 1817 as being "varied and beautiful", would also be changed. Trains, tall mill chimneys and domestic chimneys spewed out sooty smoke that fell onto the people and the buildings below, and as the sandy-coloured houses, mills and chapels were coated with layers of soot, the village at Luddenden Foot was gradually blackened. Evidence of a century of burning coal is still present today not only on the buildings in the valley but also on buildings and drystone walls on the hillsides.

The Calder, once a clean river, was now filthy. Once used to provide power to turn wheels, it was now used for waste disposal. The 1865 Royal Commission on River Pollution said that, "The Rivers Aire and Calder throughout their whole course are abused, obstructed, and polluted (to an extent scarcely conceivable by other than eye witness) from Skipton on the Aire, from Todmorden on the Calder down to Castleford" … "poisoned, corrupted and clogged by refuse from mines, chemical works, dyeing, scouring and fulling worsted and woollen stuffs, skin cleansing and tanning, slaughterhouse garbage and the sewerage of towns and houses."[9]

Pollutants dumped in the Calder upstream would flow down past Luddenden Foot and any pollutants added there would increase the load arriving at Sowerby Bridge.

The village in 1861

1. Red Lion
2. Beer House
3. Chatburn and Jennings[10]
4. Anchor and Shuttle
5. Black Lion[11]

Around the 1850s, according to Greenwood, the mill at the foot of the Lud, Luddenden Foot Mill, was known as Delph Mill. He says there were a few cottages in front of a small cotton mill which was owned by Messrs. Horsfall, Sutcliffe and Hoyle. Behind the mill were a joiner's business and a blacksmith's shop and further back still was Eli Alderson's cartwright shop.[12]

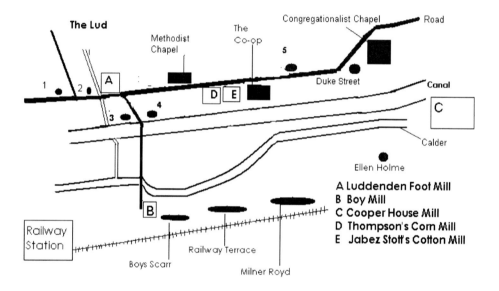

Having attracted workers to the village by providing employment, the Whitworths were faced with a housing shortage and so they, and others, built houses. The rent the workers paid was the return on their investments.[13] By 1861[14] more houses had been built in the Denholme area and there were new houses at Milner Royd, Railway Terrace and Duke Street. Above the village, at Blackwood Hall, new houses included Albion Terrace.

Immigration

Not everyone who lived in the Luddenden Foot area in 1861 had been born there. Of the total population about 50 per cent said they were born in the local townships of Sowerby and Warley and 30 per cent said they originated from other parts of the Halifax parish.[15] As the domestic system of textile manufacturing declined, workers moved to the growing towns and villages to find work in factories.

The remaining 20 per cent of the population, 1 in 5 people, came from much further away. Cheshire, Gloucestershire and especially Warwickshire and Somerset accounted for 7.7 per cent, and Ireland (Cork, Galway, and especially Counties Mayo and Tipperary) accounted for 5.8 per cent of the population. The famine in Ireland had caused increased Irish emigration. Yorkshire, beyond the Halifax Parish, and the northeast of England accounted for 3.7 per cent and the northwest of England, mainly Lancashire, made up the remaining 2.8 per cent.

In the village, probably because there was a shortage of houses, 79 people were living as boarders. Boarding houses were crowded, and some were run by Irish people for their fellow countrymen and women.

At a house in Denholme, Sarah Hanigan was a 44-year-old Irish-born widow who earned her living as a dressmaker and by taking in boarders. She had two daughters, Mary and Ellen, aged 19 years and 17 years, both born in Ireland and now working in a local cotton mill. Living with them was an Irish-born relative, Patrick, 21 years, who worked as a labourer. Six Irish boarders also lived in the house, three men and three women, and all except one woman had found work.

In 1861 Jabez Stott was a cotton manufacturer living in the Denholme area of the village[16] and his mill was next door to the recently opened Luddenden Foot Co-operative Society. Perhaps Mary and Ellen Hanigan worked at Stott's mill.

Textile workers

In 1861, in the Luddenden Foot area, of the men who worked, 65 per cent were in textiles, and of the women who worked outside the home, 91 per cent were in textiles. They worked in woollens, worsteds and cotton. One woman said she was a silk ribbon weaver and three said they were silk spinners.

The number of wool combers in the area had fallen from 135 in 1841 to 10 in 1861 because wool combing had been mechanised. The factory system of textile production had replaced the domestic system and it caused Greenwood to remark that "... now the homes of people have been made and are kept much sweeter, by the removal of the smell of the grease and the wool from their cottages." The handloom weavers and wool combers who were losing their traditional way of life may have had other concerns.

Recruitment of labour

Possibly because there was a shortage of labour in the village, the Whitworths were recruiting young people, mostly from the southwest of England, to work in their mill. In 1861 Cooper House Boys' Home housed 45 boys of whom 37 were 14 years old and 8 were 15 years old. They lived under the supervision of a governor and a governess and were described as "apprentices". They worked as worsted spinners apart from two who were oilers. For 10 of the boys their place of birth was unknown. Of the rest 22 were born in Somerset, 3 in Gloucestershire, 3 in London, 6 in Worcester and 1 in Liverpool.[17]

In a house at Ellen Holme, which was next door to Cooper House Mill, there were 19 female boarders who were aged between 12 years and 25 years and, except for one, they were born in Bristol. They were working as worsted spinners.

Education

John Turner was a woollen manufacturer whose family had run Longbottom Mill until it was taken over in 1864 by the Whitworths. In 1861 he lived with his wife and two sons at Stansfield Hall, which is across the main road from the fields above the mill, near Naylor Lane. One son was 16 years old and employed as a bookkeeper and the other, a 9-year-old, was a scholar. Turner also had a 12-year-old daughter who was a scholar.[18]

In 1861 another woollen manufacturer, James Clay, was living near the village at Middle Foot. Around that time he was only employing 55 people at Luddenden Foot Mill but his family would go on to run a huge textile concern in the village. He was married with two sons aged 10 years and 9 years and a daughter aged 1 year. Both boys were scholars.

The children of these middle-class parents, boys and girls, got an education.

Warley Grammar School

From 1786 to 1894 there was a school at Friendly which for a time was known as Spring Gardens School. Later it was called Warley Grammar School. The two houses at Spring Gardens and the next-door building, now an outdoor clothing shop, formerly a branch of Luddenden Foot Co-op, made up the original school buildings.

In 1786 the first trustees of the school were five local men. They were: Joseph Charles Gautier of Hoyle House who was a merchant, Samuel Milne who was also a merchant, James Crosley[19] of Lower Hollings who was a woollen manufacturer, Isaac Ogden who owned and lived for a long time at Upper Longbottom and John Lea of Sowerby. Lea's daughter married Joseph Priestly of White Windows who ran the fulling mill at Longbottom.

The school was "for and at all time for ever to be used and enjoyed for the better instruction of children from time to time residing within the township of Warley". Over the school door a large stone carried the inscription, "Train up a child in the way he should go, and when he is old he will not depart from it." When the school closed in 1894 the stone was moved to the Friendly Methodist Sunday school at the chapel next door. The present occupiers of the chapel have looked for the stone but unfortunately they were unable to find it.

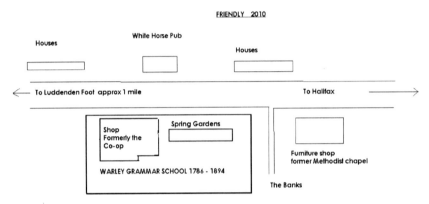

The school survived on subscriptions and loans from the trustees and others. It was always a grammar school and at times it was a boarding school. It took a number of free scholars, and scholars were of both sexes. One of the early pupils at the school was Joshua Murgatroyd, one of the twelve children of Squire Murgatroyd of Upper Longbottom.[20]

Village schools

In the 1860s for the children of better-off parents, schooling was important but for children of poor parents earning money was essential. By the age of eight most poor children in the area were at work. However, the 1833 Factories Act required that every child between 9 years and 12 years had 2 hours schooling a day and they were not to work for more than 9 hours a day. Children under 9 years were not to be employed. The 1844 Factories Act required that every child receive 3 hours schooling a day and they were not to work more than 6½ hours a day. But now 8-year-olds were allowed to work in factories. Mill children between 8 years and 13 years came to be known as "half–timers", spending either the morning or the afternoon in school, and this system of part-time education for working children was not significantly changed until the 1918 Education Act.

Greenwood mentioned two schools in the Luddenden Foot area.[21] He said that "in the village there was for a long number of years a dame's school and many of the very young children there received the first rudiments of education in the homely cottage school." Dame Schools charged a few pence a week and gave basic lessons in reading and writing. Anyone could set up these schools and the teachers needed no formal qualifications. He also wrote about a school which many youths attended "on the Sowerby side of the village kept by Mr John Mitchell, through whom they received a good education, which gave great credit to their teacher."[22] In 1861 John Mitchell lived at 12 Lane Side, Sowerby with his wife and three children.[23]

Since 1832 the Methodists in Denholme had been running a school for mill children in the basement of their chapel, but in 1860, when they were debt-free, they wanted to build a better school behind the chapel. They needed to raise £250 and John Whitworth, himself a Congregationalist, promised half the cost of the building if the remainder was raised by public subscription. Amongst the subscribers were Thomas Sykes, Thomas Greenwood and John Birtwhistle, which are names which crop up again in connection with the establishment of a Co-operative Society in the village. It wasn't until 1879 that the money was finally raised and the Local Board passed plans for the Methodists to build their new school.

According to Greenwood, before 1850 there was another school for half-timers in the village. He writes about "the old mill-like structure in Denholme belonging to Mr Eli Scott being at one time a very busy place". Part of it was used as a malt kiln, another part was used for manufacturing and part was called the old schoolroom, "half-timers from the mill being there educated". The schoolroom was the village meeting place and it was where the Luddenden Foot brass band had their practice rooms. It was in the old schoolroom, a cellar-like room that the Congregationalists of the village met. They started their services in September 1851, and used the place until their church was ready in 1859."[24]

The Congregationalists

The Independents at Booth provided services for the Congregationalists in Luddenden Foot until their chapel was ready. The chapel, paid for by John Whitworth and his brother William, was built at top o' Denholme (the top of the Denholme area). Built to impress, it cost between £5,000 and £6,000.[25] At the front of the chapel, in the centre, the building rises to become a clock tower that housed a single bell which was tolled to summon villagers to services.

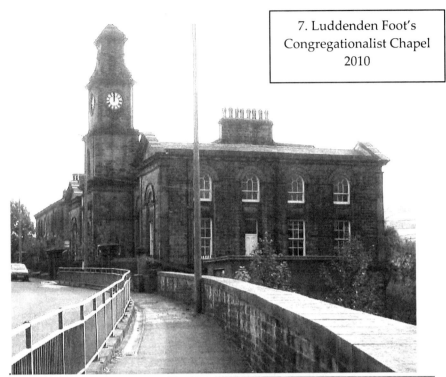

7. Luddenden Foot's Congregationalist Chapel 2010

8. Boulder Clough Chapel sits on the Sowerby hillside, top left above the long row of houses, Finkle Street. Swamp Mill was, and Swamp reservoir still is, at the far end of Finkle Street. 2010

Workers in the area who had once worked in the relative freedom of their own cottages were now subjected to the discipline of working together for long regular hours in the mills. One of the requirements of the mill owner was good time-keeping and the chapel clock, visible from many points in the Luddenden Foot area, would have enabled workers to have always known what the time was. Later Whitworths used their mill buzzer to indicate when workers should be starting or finishing work.

There were sizeable additions on each side of the chapel, one of which was the manse. The chapel survives but has been adapted for use as residences

Because there was a need to provide education for their half-timers, the Whitworths built an upper part for religious services and a lower part suitable for use as a school. Greenwood wrote that the new school would have been a great improvement on "the cellar-like" room in Denholme.

The chapel preached sobriety and the Temperance Society had its meetings there.[26] Women were prominent in the Temperance Movement because when they were married with children they were totally dependent on their husbands' wages. If their husbands spent their money at the village pubs the result for families was misery.

With the memory of hard times in the 1840s and a desire for a more secure future for themselves and their children, the congregation at the chapel saved their spare money. In 1860, a savings bank was started at the school and the trustees were John Whitworth, John Turner and William Henry Thompson. The money was mostly invested with Messrs. R Whitworths.[27]

In 1859 the Rev. Arthur Hall of the Congregationalists started the Luddenden Foot Floral and Horticultural Society "to encourage the cottage gardener".[28]

Also in 1859 the first Luddenden Foot old folks' treat was held at the Congregationalist Chapel. It was a dinner for all the old folks in the area, not just chapel people, and it was an act of charity paid for by the Whitworths.

According to Greenwood, John Whitworth, who died when he was only 47 years old,[29] was well thought of in Luddenden Foot. He said of his early death that "it was one of the worst things that could have happened to the village."[30] John Whitworth died before the money to build a new school at the Methodist chapel had been raised but in 1879 his brother, William Whitworth, kept John's promise and contributed £153 10s 6d towards the project.

John Whitworth's third son, Robert (1855–1923) was as respected a figure in the village as his father had been. He became a director of Whitworth and Co. Ltd. and was a familiar sight travelling on horseback between his home in Halifax and the Luddenden Foot mills. He is remembered as a quiet man who was a member of many philanthropic societies, without ostentation, "doing good by stealth." He founded a convalescent home in Lytham for "women in need of a rest."[31]

Three other chapels

In 1861 one of the five schoolmistresses in the area lived at Butts Green, and her nephew who lived with her was the minister at Butts Green Baptist Chapel.[32] All that remains there now is the graveyard.

The Methodist chapel at Friendly was built in 1890 and, unlike the Methodist chapel in Denholme, this building has survived. It is now used as a furniture showroom.

There was also a magnificent Methodist chapel at Boulder Clough which still overlooks the valley. It is now converted to residences.

The Methodist Friendly Society[33]

In 1858 the Luddenden Foot Free Church Friendly Society was founded at the Methodist chapel in Denholme. Friendly societies were non-profit-making mutual help organisations and were poor people's way of helping each other through hard times. Because members saved regular small amounts, the society had the funds to pay out to members who were in need because of doctors' bills, funeral expenses, or unemployment. Before there was the safety net of the Welfare State, lack of money could mean ending up in the workhouse.

The society's officers met in the Sunday school on the first Friday of every month, between 8.00pm and 9.00pm, to take contributions and to make payouts. In 1875 there were 29 male contributors and 13 female contributors. Men on average were saving a shilling per month and women on average were saving sixpence per month. When they made their payment, their membership card would be marked as a receipt for the money.[34]

Village pubs

The village now had two more pubs. In 1858 the Black Lion Inn was built, and is still standing today, and in 1861 the Chatburn and Jennings was opened at the junction of Burnley Road and Station Road.[35] In 1861 there was a newsagent at the beer house[36] at the bottom of Luddenden Lane. It was run by a Mr. Horsfall who, until his retirement in 1859, had been a teacher at "the old school room".[37] Until 1859 the village post office was at the Red Lion pub.[38]

The Oddfellows

In 1834 the Hebden Bridge District of the Oddfellows had opened Loyal Rose Lodge No. 808 and their meetings had originally been held in the Murgatroyd Arms pub in Luddenden.[39] But since 1853 the Red Lion pub had been their meeting place and the Oddfellows Lodge was the village's second Friendly Society. Within certain limits each lodge was allowed to fix its own rates of contributions and sick pay. Before 1853 members paid a flat rate of contributions but after that time a system of graduated contributions was introduced, which meant that young people paid less than older people.

Amongst the many Luddenden Foot men who joined the Loyal Rose Lodge at the Red Lion in the 1850s and '60s were George Mitchell and William Gaukroger. They are remembered by the Lodge for the work they did building the row of houses appropriately called Rose Place, opposite the now Council School at top o' Denholme. As well as providing rented homes for members in the village, the houses were considered to be a good investment for the society.

The Oddfellows was a social club and Lodge meetings were well attended. Members heeded the chapel's advice to be thrifty but advice about sobriety was not taken too seriously. The rent for the meeting room was the money spent on beer and although there were strict rules of behaviour and fines for breaking the rules, there were boisterous evenings. New members had to undergo an initiation ceremony and worrying rumours suggested that this involved "branding". Initiation of new members was carried out in semi-darkness with the candidate being blindfolded and a heavy chain placed around his neck. The chain clanked as he was led around the Lodge room by various officers until he came to the place where the presiding officer was standing. When the blindfold was removed a curtain was drawn aside and the candidate found himself in front of the skeleton of a man shining out into the darkness. He also got a view of a poker in a glowing fire.[40]

The Co-op

The Chartists of the 1830s and '40s had been unsuccessful petitioning for more representation in Parliament, and so having failed to persuade the government to help them, working-class people were thinking of ways to improve their lives by helping themselves. Through running small businesses and by involvement at chapels, some villagers had acquired organisational and leadership skills and now they were to put these skills to work. Luddenden Foot, following the example set by others,[41] joined what was to become a worldwide movement, the Co-operative Movement. Villagers were to set up their own business, a shop, where one person or group of people didn't hold all the power. Their business was to be owned and controlled by all members equally and investment in the Co-op would be made by the local people who used it. Profits would be used for the benefit of members.

On May 1st 1860, at Eli Scott's mill, a public meeting was held to take the first steps towards setting up a village Co-operative Store. By May 11th it

James Dugdale,
Chairman, 1860

H. C. Tolson,
Secretary, 1860-1869.

Henry Haigh,
Committee, 1860.

John Birtwhistle,
Committee, 1860.

9. Luddenden Foot Co-op Committee members in the 1860s: James Dugdale, HC Tolson, Henry Haigh and John Birtwhistle.

had been decided that the society would be called The Luddenden Foot Industrial Co-operative Society Ltd. and members of the first committee were: James Dugdale (an engineer), Jabez Stott (a cotton manufacturer), James Mitchell, Henry Haigh (a wool sorter), Thomas Greenwood (factory management), John Birtwhistle, Daniel Carter and Richard Barnes. Henry Tolson, who was a clerk in a worsted factory, was the secretary. William Bentley, a cashier at a factory, and David Greenwood were auditors. There were three trustees: Eli Alderson, a joiner and the innkeeper at the Anchor and Shuttle, Joseph Wells, a factory manager and Thomas Sykes.[42]

The committee hoped that villagers who joined the Co-op would learn habits of "frugality and forethought." The aim of the society was: "to raise by voluntary subscriptions a fund for better enabling its members to purchase food, firing, clothes, and other necessities of daily life – to place within the reach of the inhabitants of the area genuine goods at reasonable prices." There was a membership fee of one shilling and start-up capital was to be raised in £1 shares which members, if necessary, could pay at sixpence a week. There would be 5 per cent interest on all paid-up shares and on all borrowed money. By August 10th the code of rules was registered with the Registrar of Friendly Societies and in August 1860 Eli Scott's premises were purchased for £800 with a mortgage of £700. The society started trading in one part of the building and other parts were let off to a tinner, a plumber and to a firm of brewers. The original hours of business were 7.30am until 9.00pm except on Fridays and Saturdays when the shop stayed open until 10.00pm. They sold flour, groceries, meat and coal. In the early days credit was allowed for two weeks but by 1866 it was only allowed on coal for four months.

Dividend was paid on purchases and when "divi" day had arrived, or the half-yearly meeting was due according to Greenwood, "It was the custom to send around the village the bellman to announce that those things were about to take place." The balance sheet for the half-year ending June 29th 1861 shows that a fee of one shilling was paid to the bellman for calling the Christmas meeting.

At meetings there was an interesting method of voting to ensure that all members, no matter how much they had invested in the society, had equal voting power. When nominations had been made for men to serve on the committee, Greenwood recalled, "as many caps as there were candidates were placed in a row, each labelled with the name of a candidate, and placed side by side near the outlet from the room. Each member, being supplied with a voting ticket, filed out of the room, passed the caps, dropped the ticket on the name he most favoured, and returned into the room by another door." [43]

Thos. Greenwood,
Chairman, 1861.

James Clayton,
Chairman, 1864-1867.

John Jackson,
Committee, 1862.

John Broadbent,
Committee, 1862.

10. Luddenden Foot
Co-op Committee
members in the
1860s: Thomas
Greenwood, James
Clayton, John
Jackson, and John
Broadbent

11. Denholme Cottages, later renamed Co-operative Buildings

In 1863 the Co-op decided to build twelve houses on the land opposite their store. Workers co-operating to build their own houses was a step towards gaining some independence from private landlords. They bought the land for £120, and by 1864 the houses had been built at a cost of £1,185.[44] Because of limited space in the valley bottom, the houses were built "under-over." Each house had only one entrance. The doors to the "over" houses were found by going up the steps which were at the side of the block. The "under" houses, being "back-to-earth", would have been prone to damp and poor ventilation as well as having dark back rooms. There was a shared outside toilet block at the end of the row but this was later moved round the back because it was "a nuisance". The houses were originally called Denholme Cottages but later renamed Co- operative Buildings.

In 1868 the Co-op at Luddenden Foot became a member of The North of England Wholesale Society at Manchester (C.W.S.).

Their building had a narrow escape on Easter Monday 1870 when the cotton mill next door, owned by Jabez Stott, was destroyed by fire. Greenwood wrote that, "When the fire had been raging for some time, the roof falling in

39

pushed the gable end into the Rochdale canal. A woman on the other side of the valley was anxiously watching the progress of the fire, and, when the end tumbled down into the water she threw up her hands and exclaimed 'T'Co-op's saved!' And so it was." [45]

The Co-op organised social events for the education and enjoyment of its members and in 1866 there was a trip to Liverpool. But according to Greenwood "a rumour was current in the village that cholera was raging in Liverpool, hence only a few ventured to visit the place, but these said they heard nothing of the disease whilst there".[46]

---

[1] WYAS WYC: 1219/14.

[2] Greenwood, 18.

[3] WYAS WYC1219/14.

[4] Jennings, *Pennine Valley*, 163.

[5] Greenwood, 18, 19.

[6] Greenwood, 28.

[7] Bentley, *The Pennine Weaver*, 52.

[8] Webster, *Textiles and Tools Nineteenth Century Industry in Calderdale*, 36.

[9] *The British Medical Journal* Nov. 30 1929, 997. " *River Pollution*" quote from 1865 Royal Commission on River Pollution, x and xi.

[10] Established 1861.

[11] Established 1858.

[12] Greenwood, 39.

[13] Houses owned by Whitworths in theLuddenden Foot District by the early 1900s included: Cooper House Boys' Home, Narrow Nick, Duke Street, Ellen Holme, Milner Place, Spring View, Bank View, Prospect Terrace, Winter Neb and properties at Blackwood Hall. LFUDC minutes.

[14] 1861census returns.

[15] Wadsworth, Stansfield, Langfield, Erringden, Heptonstall, Soyland, Norland, Barkisland, Greetland, Rishworth, Ovenden, Halifax, Northowram, Elland, Shelf, Hipperholme, Brighouse, Rastrick, Fixby.

[16] 1861 census returns.

[17] 1861 census returns.

[18] 1861 census returns.

[19] Spelt with one "s".

[20] HW Harwood, "Warley Grammar School", *Trans. Halifax Antiq. Soc. Jan 1967*.

[21] Greenwood, 35.

[22] Greenwood, 34.

[23] 1861 census returns.

[24] Greenwood, 23.

[25] WYAS WYC 1219/14.

[26] *Halifax Courier*, Saturday 18 April 1874.

[27] Greenwood, 24.

[28] Greenwood, 24.

[29] WYAS HB 70.

[30] Greenwood, 33.

[31] *Halifax Guardian*, Sat May 5 1923.

[32] 1861 census returns.

[33] " Friendly Society" not to be confused with the place called "Friendly" which was in the Luddenden Foot area. Although at Friendly there is a pub called "The Friendly" which may have been so called because it ran a Friendly Society.

[34] WYAS HB:77.

[35] Demolished in 1925 to widen the road and replaced by public toilets.

[36] Later known as the Weaver's Arms pub.

[37] Greenwood, 23.

[38] The Red Lion became The General Rawdon.

[39] In the Luddenden valley, Oddfellows also had lodges at The Travellers' Rest and The Cati'th Well.

[40] WYAS MISC: 227.

[41] For example: Rochdale 1844, Todmorden 1847, Hebden Bridge 1848.

[42] Names from Greenwood, 43. Occupations from census returns.

[43] Greenwood, 53.

[44] Greenwood, 57.

[45] Greenwood, 63.

[46] Greenwood, 58.

Chapter 4
The Luddenden Foot Local Board of Health

In rapidly growing cities like Liverpool the poorest people had to live in overcrowded, damp, ill-ventilated homes with no clean water supply and no proper sewage disposal systems. The slums they lived in stank and so it was originally thought that cholera and typhoid were caught by breathing infected air. But it was later realised that the diseases were water-borne, caused by water supplies being polluted with sewerage. The government eventually took action to reduce the risk of epidemics by setting up Local Boards of Health and this was the beginning of our system of local government. There was some self-interest on the part of the ruling classes because they too were at risk when there were outbreaks of cholera and typhoid.

Local boards were made up of people who were elected by owners of property and ratepayers. In 1868 in Luddenden Foot the original Local Board members were: Joseph Greenwood (cotton manufacturer), James Clay (woollen manufacturer), W. Horsfall (cotton spinner and manufacturer), Mr. Murgatroyd (farmer of 10 acres), Mr. Radtliffe (mill-owner), Jabez Stott (cotton manufacturer), W.H. Thompson (corn miller), George Thompson (corn miller), J.W. Whitworth (manufacturer), Joseph Wells (textile factory manager), Mr. Ackroyd, Mr. Abotson and Mr. Bennet.[1] In March 1868 they appointed Thomas Farrar, who was a surveyor of highways, as the Surveyor and Nuisance Inspector. The Board, all men and mostly local manufacturers, held their meetings in the Congregationalist Chapel schoolroom.

Under Local Boards the state brought together responsibility for: the paving of streets, drainage, the safe disposal of household waste, sewage disposal, a clean water supply, burials, dealing with overcrowding, poor quality housing and the provision of public baths. Although conditions were much worse in crowded cities and towns than they were in villages, there were problems there too. In Luddenden Foot in the 1860s sanitation as we know it today didn't exist.

The Calder, once as clean and clear as any river in the Dales, was now thoroughly polluted. But when the Aire and Calder Conservancy Bill came before Parliament in February 1871, the board signed a petition to oppose it. They said that the bill "was against the interests of the district and the rate payers".[2]

Village streets were littered with waste from the horses that worked on the roads. There were stables with associated manure heaps amongst the houses in the village.

The walkways were not flagged pavements. They were dusty in dry weather and, because there was no proper surface drainage, mud pools in wet weather.

Where there was no domestic drainage, liquid domestic waste would be thrown into the street.

Shared areas for household waste, ashpits, contained ashes from domestic coal fires and other rubbish. Waste, mainly vegetable matter, would lie in foul-smelling rotting piles attracting flies.

Privies were mainly middens, which were basically holes in the ground with seats over them. They were emptied by the night-soil men who used horses and carts to carry their loads to farmland to be used as fertiliser. Privies in the village were in outside blocks and each privy was shared by a number of houses.

In December 1872 members of the Local Board attended a meeting with the Sanitary Authority to discuss the appointment of a Medical Officer of Health, and the following June, Dr. Thomas Britton was the first to be appointed to the post. He was to regularly inspect the district to identify potential causes of disease and he was to ensure that the residents had supplies of clean water. Luddenden Foot's water supply at the time came mainly from springs and wells.[3]

In October, 1873, Dr. Britton drew attention to "the fouling of water in a well at Spring Gardens, Friendly, arising from the drainage of certain piggeries running into it".

In August 1874 it was decided that any cases of smallpox or other infectious diseases that may arise in the district would be catered for in the Halifax Fever Hospital.

Women's work

By 1871[4] in the Luddenden Foot district, of the men who worked, 64 per cent worked in textiles and of the women who worked, outside the home, 88 per cent worked in textiles. Of the textile workers about 1 in 10 were between the ages of 8 and 12 years.

In 1871 in Luddenden Foot's textile mills young women worked in the less skilled occupations. They were employed as: scutchers (cleaning cotton before it was spun), slubbers (producing yarn), spinners (doffers, drawers, twisters, winders, and doublers), weavers and burlers (picking out knots and lumps in finished cloth). Women were excluded from supervisory jobs such as overlooking, jobs that required long apprenticeships such as wool-sorting, technical jobs and clerical work. Men trained for and took the better-paid jobs because when women married they were expected to spend their lives as full time housewives and mothers and as such they would be dependent on their husbands' wages. In the Luddenden Foot district, even if there were no children, the majority of wives stayed in the home.[5]

Home and family were the warp and weft of working-class married women's lives: they produced and nurtured the workforce. The cleaning, washing, shopping, cooking, mending, and rearing of often large numbers of children would have provided work for at least one full-time worker in the home. In small, damp, often overcrowded houses, with limited access to water, limited lighting, shared outside toilets and fly-infested ashpits, the struggle against dirt and disease must have been a wearying experience. The housewife would have had none of today's labour-saving devices. Victorian middle classes declared that cleanliness was next to Godliness and if you had running water, a connection to the sewers and one or two domestic servants, cleanliness would have been achievable. But if you had none of these things you may well have been considered to be one of the "great unwashed".

The growth of the village

By 1871 the population of the Luddenden Foot district was edging towards 3,000, and 1078 people lived in the village. There were 206 houses with an average of five people per house. There was some serious overcrowding and many people lived as boarders. A house in Denholme had 12 inhabitants, three family members and nine boarders. A house in Ellen Holme had two families living there, 13 people in all, and at Milner Royd, small back-to-back houses, one house had a family of 11 plus three boarders.

Houses had been built at Prospect Terrace. A row of three houses, they were built on the roadside just above the Congregationalist Chapel, which at the time was on the edge of the village. Set back off the road, these were large-roomed, "through"[6] houses with front gardens. One of them was occupied by a master dyer and his family, plus his brother-in-law, a woollen manufacturer. Another was occupied by an officer of the Inland Revenue and his family and the third by a factory manager and his family.

Houses for millworkers had been built at Narrow Neck (also known as Narrow Nick). They perched on a narrow strip of land between the Rochdale Canal and the River Calder below the Congregationalist Chapel, near Cooper House Mill. Here families lived in "one-up, one-down" cottages sharing outside toilets which were at either end of the row.[7] Most people looking at the footprint of the aptly named Narrow Neck would find it hard to believe that there was enough room to build there and would be alarmed at the thought of bringing their children to live in such a dangerous place. The houses were still inhabited in the 1950s.

In 1882 a Working Men's Club was opened in the village and for many years it was in the building which is now the Brandy Wine public house on Station Road.

In May 1886 the Victoria Hotel replaced the Anchor and Shuttle pub.

12. The Victoria Hotel building still stands on Burnley Road. It is shown here decorated for the silver jubilee of King George V in 1935. The canal is behind and Luddenden Foot UD Council offices are on the left (now demolished).

Village gas supply

Greenwood described the village in 1860 as a "quiet and sleepy" place but he added that "it was a dull dark place during the long winter months". In 1861[8] one villager said he was a "gas maker" and his work would have been at the gas-making plant near Wood Bottom Dye Works. Previously the gas works had been in the yard at Cooper House Mill but the Whitworths had moved it when they took over the mill. Greenwood said, "For a number of years they supplied the village and the surrounding district with their gas at a charge of 6s per 1000 feet net." In 1866 a number of gas lamps were put up in the village streets and they were lit for the first time on November 26th. That evening the Luddenden Foot brass band paraded the village to celebrate the occasion.[9] In August 1869 the Local Board set up a lighting committee with instructions to "superintend the management and repairs of the gas lamps in the district" and in the September they decided that "William Crabtree be reappointed lighter of the gas lamps at a weekly rate of 8 shillings". There must have been some trouble with the local youth because in January 1871 the Local Board moved that, "A hundred bills be printed giving notice that anyone found throwing stones at the gas lamps and breaking the glass will be prosecuted as the law directs."

In 1886 the gas supply at Luddenden Foot was added to by gas from the Sowerby Bridge works.[10] Gas mains were then being laid throughout the district.

The Church of England and education

13. St Mary's church on the Sowerby Hillside at Blackwood Hall above Luddenden Foot village. Bottom right is the bridge over the Calder which led to the railway station. The photograph was taken in the 1930s.

Before 1870 the state took no responsibility for providing education. However in 1870, where there was a need, the Elementary Education Act permitted Local Boards to provide schools which would be paid for by local ratepayers. But Anglicans were opposed to the undenominational religious teaching which was to be offered in Board Schools[11] and in September 1870, building began, at a cost of £1,971, on a Church of England National School at Blackwood Hall. When the school was ready, religious services were held there until the church, St Mary the Virgin, was completed in 1873. The church was paid for by four sisters, Mrs. Bean of Sowerby Parsonage and the three Misses Rawson of Haugh End,

Sowerby, and they built it as a memorial to their parents.[12] The lofty spire of St. Mary's could be seen from quite a distance when entering the village by the main road from Mytholmroyd. The school is now a private residence but the church has been demolished although the graveyard is still there.

The Catholic community

Luddenden Foot had a substantial Irish Catholic community and they held their religious services in the Co-op Hall until their church, St Walburga's, was built in 1897. [13] Their church was on Burnley Road above Prospect Terrace, opposite the Church of England vicarage.

The Old Folks' Treat

In 1859 the village's first old folks' treat, a dinner, had been given by John Whitworth in the Congregationalist Chapel schoolroom and the dinners continued until 1879. From 1879 to 1890 it was a tea given in the schoolroom around Christmas time, but after 1890 the date was changed to April because the weather was more pleasant at that time of year. The treat was for all those who were over sixty who lived in the district. Each year about a hundred and fifty people were catered for. The menu was always: roast beef, mutton, tongue and ham, followed by fancy confectioneries, and after the meal each person was given two oranges and a quarter pound of tea. In the 1880s the meat carvers included Mr. Whitworth, Mr. Clay, Mr. Murgatroyd, Mr. Tolson and Mr. Dugdale and their wives waited on tables. In the early years after the meal there was often a talk given by a local clergyman and in 1881 the talk was given by the Rev. Hopkins of Cross Lanes. He remarked on the many changes seen by the old folks during their lifetime, for instance, there had been no railways when they were young. He joked that, "It was formerly the custom for persons travelling from England to Scotland by coach to make their will before starting." He went on: "Now steam is applied to machinery and ships and by means of electricity we are able to speak to our American brethren." By 1885, after the dinner, there was entertainment which may have been a pianist, a singer, a ventriloquist or the Sowerby handbell ringers.[14]

A new building for the Co-op

In 1872, according to Greenwood, it was decided that the village Co-op needed "more up-to-date shops on a level with Burnley Road ... instead of being confined in cellar-like rooms." They also wanted a hall which could be used by the villagers for educational and social events. In March 1873 plans for a new store with a hall above it were approved by the Local Board and the building was to cost £1,750. Work started later that year and while it was going on the business was transferred to a room in Thompson's corn mill which was next door to the Co-op.[15]

14. In 1872 a branch of Luddenden Foot Co-op was opened on the Sowerby hillside at High Lee Green

By April 1874 the shops were ready and stocked up for the opening. The half-yearly dividend for members had been announced and was to be paid on April 25th. But on April 18th the villagers were shocked to read in the Saturday morning papers that Messrs. R Whitworth and Co. of Cooper House Mill had suspended payments and filed a petition of bankruptcy. The Co-op was in a difficult position because they used the firm as their bankers and they still had several contractors' accounts to pay as well as the bills for stocking up the new shop. R Whitworth and Co. also had the money needed for the dividend which was due.

When Messrs. R. Whitworth and Co. failed, they had £2,940 of the Co-op's money but the Co-op only recovered £1,059. Greenwood wrote that it was doubtful whether the society could survive the crisis but it did "by careful and prudent management and by the forbearance of its creditors."

The savers in the bank at the Congregationalist Chapel, who had also invested in the now bankrupt firm, ultimately had their investments made good from money raised by subscriptions. Mr. J. W. Whitworth, eldest son of John Whitworth contributed £3, 850. [16]

15. Luddenden Foot Co-op. Photograph taken in 1910

In 1876 the Co-op bought some land at Blackwood Hall called the Band Walk from the Whitworths and in 1886 they built four houses there, which were then sold to members.[17] In 1888 six more houses were built and the name was changed from the Band Walk to Booth House Terrace.

In 1887 the Co-op bought three fields at Morley Hall because they wanted to keep their cattle there. In those days meat was sourced locally and there were many small abattoirs in the area. In 1891 the Co-op used the land to build six houses, which were then sold to members.[18]

More problems for the Whitworths

Disaster struck the Whitworths again in 1877. At 1.00am on Wednesday morning April 11th, villagers were woken by the roar of Cooper House Mill's buzzer which was sounding because there was a massive blaze at Boy Mill.[19] As people watched the fire they knew their jobs were gone.

Longbottom Mill was now owned by John Whitworth's son, Joseph Whitely Whitworth, who had bought the mill from his uncle, William, to form Joseph W. Whitworth Ltd.[20] In 1880 just before Christmas on December 23rd, a severe storm caused flooding at Luddenden Foot and Longbottom Mill was damaged when water entered the weaving sheds, forcing the end wall out of the oldest one.

A new bridge across the Calder

At the same time, in the village centre, the old stone bridge across the Calder and the road to the railway station were destroyed. At 4.45pm that day William Crabtree and a fellow mill worker, Howard Sykes, noticed a crack in the stonework and went to inspect it but when they were on the bridge they felt it sway and got off just in time to see it collapse into the river.[21] The *Halifax Courier* reported the flooding, saying "... the people of the village were alarmed when the water of the Calder rose high on Wednesday evening ..." They added that the Local Board disclaimed ownership of the bridge, saying, "... they thought that the Lancashire and Yorkshire Railway Co. would throw a temporary bridge over the breach."[22] A temporary wooden bridge was put up until a permanent replacement could be built.[23]

16. Built in 1882, the bridge over the Calder at Luddenden Foot. 2010

In February 1881, the Local Board asked for subscriptions towards repairing the bridge and the Lancashire and Yorkshire Railway Company contributed £1,625 towards the cost of widening the road from Burnley Road to the station and building a new iron bridge over the Calder.

In October 1882, when the new bridge was completed, the Local Board instructed the engineer to "get two lamps suitable to the structure of the bridge to be placed thereon ... and to put a proper inscription on the bridge which shall contain the names of the members who have been on the Board since the construction of the bridge, such inscription to be placed on the parapet of the bridge."

The men who built the bridge but whose names don't appear on the inscription were: Samuel Uttley (engineer), Messrs. Wood Brothers of Sowerby (the ironwork), James Wied of Luddenden Foot (mason) and Messrs. Thomas and sons of Hebden Bridge (painters). The bridge they built is as impressive as any in Calderdale, although it is in need of a coat of paint.

The Mechanics' Institute

In 1870 the Co-op had opened a news room which gave villagers access to newspapers. But in 1885 it was closed because it was "greatly abused by some lively and perhaps too frolicsome youths who frequented it."[24] The following year, on 16th September, the Rev. E. M .F. Stack, vicar of the Church of England, the Rev. J. Booth, of the Congregationalists, and the Rev. G. Mellilieu, of the Methodists, Robert Whitworth, Charles Clay and Albert Thompson, amongst others, met in the Congregationalist schoolroom. They set up a Mechanics' Institute for the young men of the village and Charles Clay provided rooms for the Institute at Bank Buildings.

Young men who had been half-timers had only limited education and employers were beginning to need people who were skilled in technology and who understood some of the science behind the machines they were using and maintaining. Mechanics' Institutes had grown up throughout the textile and manufacturing districts. In the 1840s Elizabeth Gaskell referred to them in *Mary Barton*, saying, "Mathematical problems are received with interest, and studied with absorbing attention by many a broad-spoken, common-looking factory-hand."

At the Luddenden Foot Institute the charges were: a one-shilling enrolment fee and a further two shillings per quarter to be paid in advance. Courses were offered in: geometry, building construction, botany, geology, machine construction and applied mechanics. To encourage interest in national events the Institute provided: *The Leeds Mercury*, *The Yorkshire Post*, *The Manchester Guardian*, *The London Daily News* and *The London Daily Standard*. Weekly publications included: *English Mechanic, Building News and Engineering, Public Opinion* and *Punch*. In December 1886 a library was established and some of the books were donated by William Whitworth. It was decided that "14 days be allowed for the reading of a book and the fine for non-renewal when due be 1p per week per volume." In 1887, shorthand, chemistry and elementary drawing were added to the list of classes and the Institute also proposed to have a Conversationalist Society or Discussion Class. When special lectures were given they took place in the Co-op hall, and on these occasions ladies were invited to sell tickets.[25]

Sanitation

In 1888 the estimated population of the Luddenden Foot district was 2,850, the birth rate was 27.7 per 1000 and the death rate was 13.7 per 1000. The Medical Officer of Health commented on the extremely low death rate saying that it compared "most favourably with other districts and had continued for several years". He attributed the absence of typhoid to "the bed of the Calder, so much fouled and exposed in the upper parts of its course, in this district being covered by water, six inches to three foot, due to the presence of two weirs below the bridge."[26]

But in January 1889 he complained about "inadequate privy provision in the main street of Luddenden Foot ... one privy and one ashpit for eleven houses."

In November 1889 he wanted the Local Board to take on the regular collection of domestic waste. He said the ashpits "were in a very offensive and unhealthy state and the nuisance will continue to a great extent so long as occupants have to see to the emptying and would it not be possible for the Local Board to take on the scavenging, say on the Goux or tub system which works well in Halifax ... or enforce the emptying every four or at least six months?"

In September 1892 the Local Boards of Midgley, Warley and Luddenden Foot united to form the Luddenden Hospital Board District and they planned to build their own hospital for the treatment of infectious diseases. In December they bought Moor Bottom Farm in Warley for the hospital site and in April 1893 a procession was planned for the occasion of laying the foundation stone. It was decided that if any patients belonging to the Luddenden Foot board were to suffer from smallpox, they would be admitted to the hospital free of charge.

Village Businesses

In the early 1890s Crowther and Son, Surgeons, the village doctors, were based in one of the large houses which were attached to the Congregationalist Chapel.[27] Other businesses in the village included a branch of the Halifax Joint Stock Banking Co. Ltd., a post office, and a newsagent's shop. There were builders, carpenters, plumbers, painters, wheelwrights, blacksmiths, saddlers, coal merchants, clog makers, shoemakers, drapers, tailors, dressmakers and hairdressers. The Co-op was housed in one of the grandest stores in the valley and there were also butchers' shops, grocers and greengrocers, fried fish dealers and confectioners. Surprisingly, there was a jeweller's business.

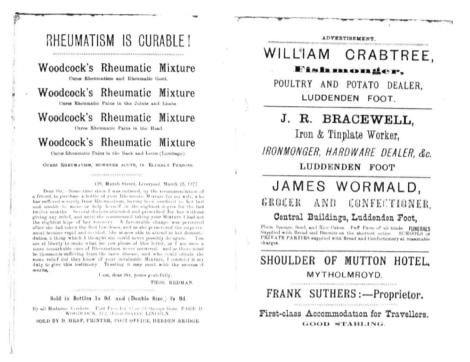

17. From an 1884 almanac

[1] Names from Luddenden Foot Local Board of Health minutes WYAS CMT11 SPL: 176. (1868-80), 177 (1880-91), 178 (1891-96). Occupations from census returns.

[2] LFBH minutes, Feb. 1871.

[3] LFBH minutes, Nov. 1894.

[4] 1871 census returns.

[5] 1871 census returns.

[6] They had two entrances - a front door and a back door.

[7] Interview with Cyril Charnley.

[8] 1861 census returns.

[9] Greenwood, 24.

[10] Jennings, *Pennine Valley*, 188.

[11] Jennings, *Pennine Valley*, 139.

[12] Kelly's Directory of the West Riding of Yorkshire 1893.

[13] Greenwood, 34.

[14] WYAS SPL 222-231.

[15] Greenwood and OS map 1888 - 93 sheet ccxxx 7 LFLBD.

[16] Greenwood, 24 and 66-68.

[17] Greenwood, 71.

[18] Greenwood, 75, 76, 79.

[19] Greenwood, 72.

[20] WYAS WYC 1219/14.

[21] *Halifax Evening Courier*, 25 May 1956, "Today's Picture".

[22] *Halifax Courier,* Sat. 1 January 1881.

[23] Greenwood, 75.

[24] Greenwood, 75.

[25] WYAS SPL 216-221.

[26] LFBH records Feb. 1888.

[27] Kelly's Directory of the West Riding of Yorkshire 1893.

Chapter 5
Towards the twentieth century

In 1893 the three main landowners in the Luddenden Foot district were the Whitworths, the Clays and the trustees of the late Major General E.A.G. Rawden of Rawden, Leeds.[1] General Rawden had one of the village pubs named after him (now called the Coach and Horses). Until 1894 it was there that the Local Board met on the second Wednesday of every month. After that time the Board was replaced by the Luddenden Foot Urban District Council.

At the turn of the century Britain was the most powerful industrial nation in the world. People working in Luddenden Foot's textile mills were better off than their grandparents had been but when jobs were lost there was no unemployment pay, when people were ill there was no National Health Service and when they were too old to work there was no old age pension. There was still only charity, poor relief and the workhouse, although workhouse regimes had become more humane because more working-class people and women were Poor Law Guardians. There were improvements in 1908 when means-tested pensions were introduced, which were from one to five shillings per week for persons over seventy. In 1911 the government took the first steps towards founding the Welfare State with the introduction of a scheme for sickness and unemployment pay for workers in industries that suffered periodic unemployment. Workers and employers paid weekly contributions into a fund for unemployment benefit which in the 1920s and '30s was known as "the dole."

Henry Sagar

On March 11th 1896 a section of Wood Bottom Dye Works was destroyed by fire, which meant a loss of employment. It was rebuilt but a few years later the firm transferred to another part of the country.[2] A young man called Henry Sagar set up in business there with J. T. Meredith and they too were dyers. By 1908 the company was listed as Henry Sagar Ltd., Cooper House, dyers and finishers. [3]

The Clays' textile mills

By the 1890s James Clay had created a hugely successful textile empire and he was a major employer in the village.[4] In 1872 Messrs Clay and Horsfall were running Luddenden Foot Mill[5] and by 1888 the Clays owned a new mill, known as Delph Mill, which was along the road from Luddenden Foot Mill just past the Coach and Horses. The Clay family also ran Boy Mill. According to Greenwood, after the fire at Boy Mill in 1877, it lay in ruins for many years until finally it was rebuilt and sold to Messrs. James Clay Ltd. The Local Board passed plans for the Clays to make additions to Boy Mill in June 1894. It was a huge mill made up of a collection of two-, three- and four-storey buildings. It lay alongside the River Calder opposite Holmes Park and it was very close to the row of houses called Boys Carr.

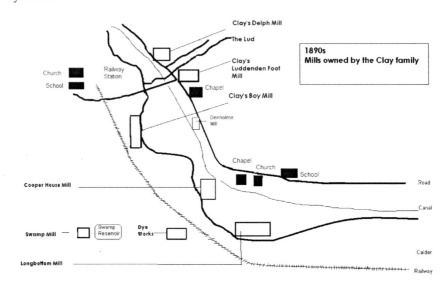

Boy Mill was managed by James's son Charles and they made worsted cloth for the fashion industry, the War Office, the Post Office, the Admiralty and the India Office. There was an export trade with Europe, America, Canada and Australia. By 1895 the Clay family's mills employed between 1,000 and 1200 people. [6]

The fire at Boy Mill

As reported in the local newspaper, Tuesday 12th April 1906 was at the start of a bad week for Messrs. James Clay &Co. Ltd. There was a fire in the carding room at Delph Mill and the room was almost destroyed. But this was a minor setback compared to what the Thursday of that week had in store. Fred Temple, a local greengrocer, was walking past Boy Mill at 5.30am when he saw smoke and suspected fire. The village fire buzzer was near the tram terminus so he rushed there to sound the alarm and by 5.50am the local fire brigade was tackling the fire. It was the older part of the mill that was on fire, the part furthest away from the railway station, where there were large weaving sheds, a drying room and a storeroom. The fire was just behind the houses at Boys Scarr

56

which were only separated from Boy Mill by the road to the mill yard. The ten families who lived there were frightened out of their beds by the fire buzzer and they did their best to protect their belongings by carrying their furniture out of their houses into the road furthest away from the fire. Once again people were gathering to watch their jobs go up in smoke. By 6.00am the mill roof had fallen in and by 6.30am the walls had fallen. But by 6.45 the Halifax Brigade had arrived and they would have arrived earlier if they hadn't met a tram at Friendly and damaged their vehicle trying to pass it. The accident had disabled the fire engine and the firemen had pulled it the rest of the way to Luddenden Foot. The newer part of the mill, nearest to the railway station, was saved but the old mill could not be saved and much of it fell into the River Calder. By 9.00am the mill was still burning but the fire was under control. The houses were safe and the people, with their belongings scattered in the road, were also safe.[7]

The fire at Boy Mill was a serious blow to local employment as about a hundred people lost their jobs. Before the fire the future of the oldest part of Boy Mill was secure but the newer part, which was unaffected by the fire, was scheduled to be demolished. At the time there was a plan to widen the railway and according to Greenwood, in 1907 the Yorkshire and Lancashire Railway Company bought and demolished the mill and so even more people lost their jobs. Many had to leave the village to seek work elsewhere."[8]

The huge Boy Mill which stood on the footprint of the ancient fulling mill was gone but the houses at Boys Scarr are still standing today.[9]

Fairlea Mill

New employment opportunities were created in 1907 when Fairlea Mill Co. Ltd. set up in the village.[10] Their business was the spinning and manufacturing of cotton and waste fabrics for sheets, bedspreads and cotton blankets. They also spun yarn for rope, twine, carpets and mops.[11]

Crossfield's Mill

In 1911 more jobs were created when another new firm opened in the village. They were J.W. Crossfields, Waste Processers, and their premises, Denholme Mills, were on Burnley Road just below the Co-op. The building still exists and is now a camping shop. The Crossfield brothers, William, Donald and Arthur, also owned a four-storey warehouse at the bottom of the village (now a two-storey residence). At the top of the village, across from the school and above Belmont Terrace, there was a garage where the firm kept its waggons. Waste processing, shoddy, was the recycling business. Old woollen cloth was ground up until it resembled the original raw material, some fresh wool was

18 Denholme Mill from Burnley Road, 2010. Further up on the same side, now covered with trees, is where the Co-op building used to be.

19. Denholme Mill from the Rochdale Canal bank. 2010

added and then cloth was produced from the mixture of the old and the new. Crossfields outsourced some work which women did in their homes to earn a few extra shillings. Small tubes which still contained bits of wool were collected from local spinning departments and delivered in large bags to the outworkers who would pick off the wool. Women would be paid a few pence for each bag of wool they filled.[12]

The rag and bone man who travelled around with his horse and cart collecting the rags people had saved in their ragbags was also in the recycling business. In exchange for their rags people would be given a small payment, which in later years may have been a yellow stone or a donkey stone. Women who took pride in their homes scrubbed the pavement outside their doors (swilled out) and they cleaned their doorsteps and windowsills. They would then yellowstone (soft sandstone) the steps and the windowsill to bring them back to their original sandstone colour and some would use a donkey stone (chalk) to neatly edge them with a white line.

The Co-op's Jubilee celebrations

It was now fifty years since the Co-op had set up in the village and so they decided to allow £60 for Jubilee celebrations. The committee gave all the children in the district a treat, which was on Saturday July 23rd. Those taking part met at the Council School at 2.30pm. The children were given a ticket for their lunch, a bag of sweets and were then marched out of the schoolyard and through the village to Morley Hall Farm. The procession was led by Sowerby Brass Band and in the procession were two decorated drays. The one belonging to Luddenden Foot Co-op was carrying C.W.S. produce. The other one belonged to Hebden Bridge Co-operative Society and it was carrying buns from their bakery for the children's lunch. Also on show was the new Luddenden Foot and Midgley ambulance carriage. The Co-op premises in Burnley Road were decorated for the occasion and in the field at Morley Hall about a thousand parents and children were served with tea and buns, and entertainment included a Punch and Judy show.[13]

Co-op membership in 1870 was 474, in 1880 it was 503, in 1890 it was 448, in 1900 it was 492 and in 1910 it was 551.

Total Sales at the Co-op for the 50 years from 1860 to 1910 were £631,107. The total paid in interest and dividends was £103,831. Greenwood considered that, "Surely the distribution of such a sum of money must have been helpful to many and must have brightened many a life and home in the locality."[14]

20. In 1910 a new branch of the Co-op was opened at Friendly, in part of the old Warley Grammar School building.

21. Co-op Jubilee Committee. 1910. Joseph Greenwood is seated front, 4th from the left. Tim Helliwell, local knurr and spel champion, is seated at the front, first left.

Education

In 1894, because of competition from the district's free elementary schools, there were only eleven children, eight boys and three girls, attending Warley Grammar School. It was decided to close the school. The property was sold and the money was used to provide scholarships for children in the Warley area. When Sowerby Bridge Secondary School (later the Grammar School) came into being, some pupils were awarded scholarships so that they could go there and when the Education Act of 1944 meant these scholarships were no longer needed, the money was used to help scholars who went to universities.[15]

By 1895 there were two schools in the district. There was St. Mary's Church of England School at Blackwood Hall and a new Board School on Burnley Road. There were 238 children enrolled at the Church of England School and at the Board School there were 293 children.[16] After 1902 Board Schools were run by Local Education Authorities and the 1918 Education Act abolished the "half-time" system.[17] When it was set up the "half-time" system had ensured that factory children received some schooling after the age of eight, but now there was a desire to increase and improve the education offered to children.

From 1906 until 1937 evening classes were available in the village for young people who had left school and who wanted to continue learning. Some of the classes were at the Council School and some were at the Mechanics' Institute. During this period different subjects were offered to boys and girls. The subjects on offer were suggestive of the different roles the children would be playing in their adult lives. Boys were offered: English, arithmetic, drawing and woodwork. Girls were offered: English, house management, cookery, needlework and dressmaking.

The Workers' Education Association (WEA) was active in the village trying to popularise adult education. By 1919 they were running evening classes in economics for people who were keen to learn and who would turn up to study in gaslit classrooms after a day's work.

In the early 1900s there was a serious lack of interest in learning and a worrying financial position at the Mechanics' Institute. But in 1912 one activity there that was thriving was billiards. Unfortunately, following a match against Mytholmroyd there was a complaint against the less than sportsmanlike behaviour of the Luddenden Foot lads. There had been a "snuff blowing incident." A written apology was sent to Mytholmroyd, with regret that such a thing could happen, and there was an offer to replay the match. The billiard league secretary was to be acquainted with the matter.[18]

The First World War

Tragically, two years later, many of Luddenden Foot's fun-loving young men would leave their village to fight and in some cases to die in the horrors of the First World War. After the war the committee at the Institute reported that, "A list of members had been prepared who had served in the war and that the number was ninety-seven, ten of whom had made the greatest sacrifice. It was proposed to erect a suitable memorial on the premises as a tribute to all these members".[19] The churches and chapels of the district had their own memorials to the members they had lost in the war.

The 1914 -1918 war claimed the lives of sixty-three men from Luddenden Foot.

In 1921 it was decided that a suitable commemoration service should be held at the war memorial at each anniversary of the Armistice and a bugle was presented to the council to be sounded at the service in the playing of "The Last Post".

The cenotaph was originally at the Mount of Remembrance at Bar Wood, opposite the entrance to Daisy Bank. The entrance, with inscription, can still be seen from the roadside. The war memorial was moved in the 1950s to a new site in Holmes Park.

In a letter to the *Halifax Courier* in August 1992, Stuart Holland, who lived at Bar Wood as a child, wrote about the remembrance services and the uniformed organisations attending them. He said, "The pathways were full of people all the way up to the cenotaph which was at the very top of the gardens and it was always a moving moment when 'The Last Post' was played and the sound echoed down the valley." He went on to say that the gardens were beautifully kept and they were a favourite place for children to play. The rocks at the back of the gardens were a refuge for tramps (unemployed, homeless people). They used to spend the night there. He added "My mother would fill their billycans for them and give them slices of bread ... and she never refused any of them even though we were on rationing."[20]

The British Legion movement opened a branch in Luddenden Foot in 1922 and it was one of the first to be presented with the Legion Standard. A new headquarters was built at the bottom of Luddenden Lane in 1929.[21]

22. The cenotaph in Holmes Park, Luddenden Foot. 2010

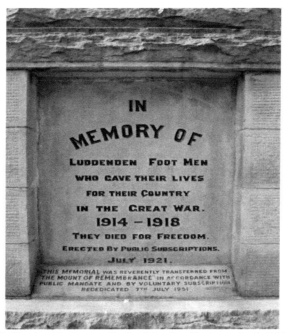

IN
MEMORY OF
LUDDENDEN FOOT MEN
WHO GAVE THEIR LIVES
FOR THEIR COUNTRY
IN THE GREAT WAR.
1914 – 1918
THEY DIED FOR FREEDOM.
ERECTED BY PUBLIC SUBSCRIPTIONS.
JULY 1921.
THIS MEMORIAL WAS REVERENTLY TRANSFERRED FROM
THE MOUNT OF REMEMBRANCE IN ACCORDANCE WITH
PUBLIC MANDATE AND BY VOLUNTARY SUBSCRIPTION
REDEDICATED 7TH JULY 1951

23. The inscription on the Luddenden Foot cenotaph. 2010

[1] Kelly's Directory of the West Riding of Yorkshire, 1893.

[2] Greenwood, 82.

[3] [3] WTC1233.

[4] Kelly's Directory of the West Riding Volume 1, 1897.

[5] LFLBH minutes, Dec. 1872.

[6] Hargreaves, *Sowerby Bridge in Old Photographs*, 80.

[7] *Halifax Evening Courier,* Thursday April 12 1906, 5 o'clock edition.

[8] Greenwood, 91.

[9] There are photographs of Boy Mill on Malcolm Bull's "Calderdale Companion" website.

[10] Greenwood, 92.

[11] WYAS WYC: 1133.

[12] Interview with Cyril Charnley.

[13] Greenwood, 84.

[14] Greenwood, 99.

[15] Harwood, "Warley Grammar School," *Trans. Halifax Antiq. Soc.* Jan 1967.

[16] WYAS T/ED 9-10, 178.

[17] Jennings, *Pennine Valley*, 139-141.

[18] WYAS SPL, 216-221.

[19] WYAS SPL, 216-221.

[20] This would be after the Second World War.

[21] Owen Sellers interview.

Chapter 6
The village between the wars

Sixty-three young men from Luddenden Foot who were cheered off to the 1914-18 war never returned to their village. Amongst the men who did survive the trenches there was a belief that there would never be another war. They thought that the world was going to be a better place and that England would build "a land fit for heroes." But this proved difficult to achieve because when trade slumped, unemployment and the dole became a feature of life for many during the '20s and '30s.

Unemployment

In 1921 there was a prolonged coal strike which caused hardship in the district, and the Whitworths, the Clays and Fairlea all helped the village by releasing coal from their stocks.[1]

In the 1920s there was a Luddenden Foot unemployment committee and they wanted to provide work for the unemployed by widening Burnley Road at Bar Wood and Warley Wood.[2] By May 1927 the West Riding County Council were preparing to go ahead with this plan. In February 1931 more work was created when a plan to widen and improve Luddenden Lane was approved.

In February 1930 jobs were lost in the village because of another mill fire. Brick Mill run by Messrs. Whiteley and Sons, which was next door to the six-storey Cooper House Mill, was completely destroyed.[3]

But in his 1933 report to the council, the Medical Officer of Health said: "The main industries are cotton spinning and doubling, worsted spinning and weaving ... Work has been more plentiful hence there has been less unemployment." In 1935 he said, "there has been little unemployment throughout the year."

Employment

Between the wars, two of the mills in the village changed hands. In the 1920s one was bought by H J Homfray and Co. Ltd. (manufacturers of rugs and carpets) and became involved in pile yarn spinning. The other was taken over by Homfray's subsidiary company, British Furtex and they manufactured upholstery fabrics.[4]

A new mill

Harry Hellewell, who was a worsted spinner, had started his business in part of Fairlea Mill but in 1924 he built Holme Royd Mill next door to Fairlea.

24. Hellewell's Mill under construction – note the horse and cart travelling along past Milner Royd and Fairlea Mill at the top of the picture.
Taken from the top of the mill chimney.

25. Looking across the valley from Railway Terrace to the Warley hillside showing the houses lining Burnley Road. On the left there is washing on the line at Robertshaw Buildings and on the far right is Duke Street to the left of the Congregationalist chapel clock.

26. Hellewell's new boiler at the base of the mill chimney.

27. Hellewell's Mill. Photograph taken from Burnley Road opposite the Black Lion pub. The row of houses behind the mill is part of Milner Royd. To the right of the chimney is Railway Terrace. Just showing on the extreme right is Boys Scarr.

28. Taken in the 1930s. One of Hellewell's spinning sheds decorated for Christmas

29. In the 1930s Hellewells proudly showed off their waggons and produce. They won two first prizes at the Infirmary gala.

In 1935 there was a fire at Hellewell's Mill and because the houses had been built so close to the mill, there was a real fear that they would be affected. The heat from the fire did crack windows in Railway Terrace.[5] The weeks after the fire were spent cleaning and renovating the spinning frames which had been damaged by water.

Luddenden Foot Mills in the 1930s

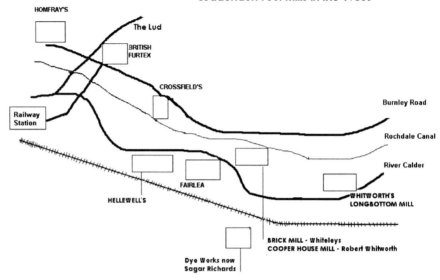

HOMFRAY'S

The Lud

BRITISH FURTEX

CROSSFIELD'S

Burnley Road

Railway Station

Rochdale Canal

River Calder

FAIRLEA

HELLEWELL'S

WHITWORTH'S
LONGBOTTOM MILL

BRICK MILL - Whiteleys
COOPER HOUSE MILL - Robert Whitworth

Dye Works now
Sagar Richards

30. The fire at Hellewell's Mill in 1935

A new boiler for Fairlea Mill

31. In the 1930s a new boiler arrives by train for Fairlea Mill

32. The boiler being man-handled into the boiler room. The row of houses on the left is Milner Royd. The mill chimney belongs to the next door mill, Hellewell's.

Transport

One of the farms on the Warley hillside was making a living supplying milk to the villagers. A member of the Kershaw Friendship Club recalled living at Upper Longbottom Farm:[6]

"Most of the work was done with a horse and cart. Luddenden Lane held all the shops to keep them in working order. The farrier's to shoe the horse, the saddler's for the harness and the tin-smith to repair the milk cans.

"Dad was often poorly so I had to do a lot of the farm work, delivering milk, etc. We had twelve to fifteen cows, a horse, hens and ducks. Dad had no dog to fetch in the cows so it was one of my jobs to go and get them. They were in the fields below Burnley Road, right down by the canal. It was a long way to drive them, up the fields, along Burnley Road and up John Naylor Lane. They walked calmly up the road, in single file, but as soon as a tram appeared, one of them always blocked the road."

By April 1901 the tram system of public transport had reached Luddenden Foot from Halifax. Later that year trams were running to Mytholmroyd and by the following year they were running to Hebden Bridge.[7] But the trams met competition from the more flexible motor buses and by March 1927 the Hebble Bus Service in Halifax were planning to run buses from Halifax to Luddenden Foot, Mytholmroyd and Heptonstall.

By the early 1900s, the motor car had made its appearance in the village although at this time car ownership was only for the well-off. Non-infectious hospital cases were usually taken to the Halifax Infirmary by motor ambulance but sometimes they were taken in the local horse-drawn ambulance which had the reputation of being "most uncomfortable." [8]

Greenwood, writing about the village in 1910, said: "...it has lost the quiet and sleepy aspect of former days. Things are now much livelier; the days of the 'buses (horsedrawn) have come and gone, the tram cars have arrived, the bicycles are spinning through the village, and the numerous motor cars of modern times are hurrying along the highway. These things have compelled the inhabitants of the dales to look around them more quickly than it was necessary in years gone by."

There was growing concern about road safety. In August 1919 a letter was received from the West Riding County Council which urged the importance of limiting the speed of motor cars passing through Luddenden Foot. There were already "Drive Slowly" signs but the council resolved to suggest a speed limit of 10mph through the village.

Because of public transport workers no longer needed to live within walking distance of their place of work. They could now live in one place and commute to work in another.

33. Showing Luddenden Foot Mill at the bottom of the village, late 1920s.

34. Traffic accident on Burnley road in Luddenden Foot. The row of houses on the left is Duke Street and behind them Mill Lane leads down to the Rochdale Canal and to Cooper House Mill which became Sagar Richards. 1930s.

Street lighting

By the 1920s the district had electricity to light the streets. By November 1921 there were 19 electric streetlights working in Boulder Clough, and by January 1922 there were 43 electric street lights in the district. Work was going on to cut off the supply to street gaslights.

Water supply

Water supply to houses in 1925 was 16 per cent Halifax Corporation, with 84 per cent made up of Sutcliffe's and Whitworths' private supplies and spring water. By 1935 water supply was 27 per cent from Halifax Corporation, 4 per cent from Sowerby Bridge UD council, 25 per cent from Whitworth's private supply and 44 per cent from springs.[9] In dry summers springs could fail

Sewage Works

35. The sewage works are in the centre, Longbottom Mill is in the foreground and Sowerby Bridge is top left. 2010

Since the early 1900s there had been a sewage works for Luddenden Foot at High Royd between the canal and the Calder below Warley Wood. This meant that wet midden closets and pail closets (which had to be emptied by the night-soil men) could be converted to the water carriage system (toilets that flush).

The conversions would take decades and a few properties never were converted.

In 1923 there were 598 privies in the district but only 184 were on the water carriage system.[10] In 1935 there were 711 privies in the district with 490 on water carriage.[11]

Because the privies were outside, those that were on the water carriage system froze in winter.

A member of the Kershaw Friendship Club recalled her childhood experiences:[12]

"Inside toilets were unheard of when I was a child. I lived in the centre of Luddenden Foot and we had to use the toilets and middens at the Co-op. You climbed fifty steps to get to them so you had to be pretty fit. There were just four toilets, with wooden seats, to share between quite a lot of families. Every family had its own key to the toilets. Of course at night you wouldn't trail through the village to go to the toilet. Everyone would use a 'go under' which was kept under the bed.

"Once a week around midnight two men would come with a horse and cart. It was their job to carry the dustbin-sized toilet buckets down the steps and empty them into the tank on their cart."

36. The Mechanics' Institute, now the Civic Centre, Luddenden Foot. 2010

The slipper baths

A new building on Station Road housed the Mechanics' Institute and also the public baths, known locally as the slipper baths. In 1915[13] when the baths were opened by County Councillor S. Dugdale, their introduction into the area was considered to be as "necessary as sewering". People had no facilities at home for bathing other than a tin bath in front of the fire but at the slipper baths for sixpence you could have a first-class bath which was: a hot bath, a hot and cold shower, two towels, soap and a brush. For threepence you could have a second-class bath which was: a hot bath, a cold shower, one towel, soap and a brush. The time allowed for each bath was 30 minutes and from July 1917 it was decided that certain bath times were to be reserved for ladies only.[14]

A Kershaw Friendship Club member recalled:[15]

"If we wanted a bath, we either had to take down the old tin bath and go to all the bother of boiling water and filling it or use the Public Baths. Once a week we all went, with our soap and towels, to the Municipal Baths on the other side of the bridge. It was under the Institute, next to the Buck Trap Inn."

Poor Housing

Too much of Luddenden Foot's housing stock was in poor repair and in January 1922 the West Riding County Council wanted an assurance that steps were being taken to remedy the housing conditions within the district. Many families rented "under-overs" and "back-to-backs" and some landlords were not keen when it came to repairing their buildings or modernising the sanitary arrangements. They were sometimes required to put their houses in order.

In the village centre there was a block which was three storeys high containing ten "under-over" houses. The houses on the ground floor were one storey high and they had only one room and a very small scullery, which was back-to-earth. The ground level at the back was twenty feet above the floors. The sculleries were damp, dark, and with no means of ventilation and it was estimated that to ventilate the sculleries would cost more than the building was worth. Although water was piped to the houses there were no sinks and the often leaking taps dripped into the bowls which were generally kept under them. In 1921 they were considered to be far from healthy houses.[16]

In June 1923 the average number of people per household in the district was 3.45 but the Sanitary Inspector reported "we have far too many overcrowded houses, in three dwellings eight persons occupy one bedroom.. Some houses were overcrowded "both morally and in number".

Warley Wood Estate

It was recognised in Luddenden Foot that in the district there was a shortage of a hundred decent houses.[17] The council planned to build "houses suitable for the working classes" on a site they had bought at Warley Wood and the initial plan was to build fifty-six houses with two, three, or four bedrooms with baths and water closets on the first floors.[18] Unfortunately only half of these houses

37. Warley Wood estate. Below the estate is Daisy Bank and bottom right is the sewage works.

had been built when the government subsidy was stopped because there just wasn't enough money. However the council decided to continue to build houses with money they hoped to raise by selling the completed ones on easy terms. This began to happen, but in 1927 house sales slowed to a halt. A report to the council in May 1927 said: "There have been no further sale of houses and the three are still unsold. It is rather surprising when one takes into consideration the splendid and healthy position of the house. It has three bedrooms, scullery, living room, bathroom, and parlour with bay window, hot and cold water, gas and electricity, with a nice plot of land front and back. They are very convenient, and the price is £520, which is £110 less than they cost."[19]

Throughout the '20s and '30s in Luddenden Foot, efforts were made to improve the existing housing stock and to build modern homes but in July 1928 it was admitted by the council that "the number of houses built in the last few years does not appear to have relieved the overcrowding." There was still much inadequate housing.

Health care
One of the new houses at Warley Wood became the district nurse's house. There had been a district nurse in Luddenden Foot since 1913 when a resident of the district provided money to finance one. He also left enough money in his will to finance a Nursing Institute for five years. Until 1938 the Institute was kept going by voluntary donations and fund-raising socials but after 1938 a Provident

Contributary Scheme was introduced with each householder agreeing to pay 1d per week to become a member.[20]

In the early 1930s there were a number of outbreaks of two of the infectious diseases of the time, scarlet fever and diptheria, with nearly all cases of the diseases being in children of school age.[21] The council's Sanitary Inspector reported that the outbreaks had occurred despite improvements in drainage and sewering, a large number of conversions to the water carriage system, satisfactory removal of household refuse, streets being cleaned, new houses being built, other properties being brought up to a better standard, and sanitary conditions in schools being excellent.

In 1935, a maternity and child welfare centre was opened in the Mechanics' Institute building in the village. Previously mothers had to go to Sowerby Bridge or Hebden Bridge.[22]

A Kershaw Friendship Club member spoke harsh words about the experience of some women at this time:

"Women were downtrodden, just slaves for their men-folk. By the time they'd finished having their babies all they were fit for was sitting by the fire like old women!"

A vibrant village community

In the 1920s and '30s the village of Luddenden Foot was a vibrant community and people's needs were mostly catered for locally by the many businesses and shops which lined Burnley Road.

One of the more modern shops was run by Mr. J E Kershaw at Victoria Buildings and he was a radio dealer.[23] Listening to the radio, or wireless, was a very popular form of home entertainment in the days before television, and it was possible to do this even if your house had no electricity supply. The radio was connected to a large acid-filled glass battery and when the battery was flat it could be taken to Mr. Kershaw who would exchange the flat battery for a charged one. His shop was still in the village in the 1950s when he also sold televisions.

The Catholic Church was a fun place to be on Saturdays in the '20s and '30s because the village cinema was in their basement.[24]

A Kershaw Friendship Club member recalled:[25]

"It was 2d for the front seats, 5d for the middle and 9d for the plush seats at the back. A man played the piano during the films. Boys tried to creep under the chairs at the front to get to the 5d seats but the piano player would stop playing and make them go back. Afterwards we called at Cooper's – best fish and chips in the world – and then walked home."

Another club member recalled:

"Mr Shaw, the projectionist, had a petrol driven projector which was quite apt to set on fire. I remember he once singed his goatee beard!"

38. Smith's butchers, Denholme Buildings, Luddenden Foot

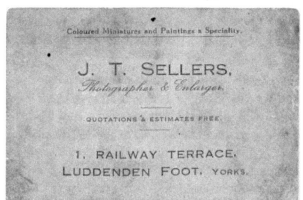

39. J. T. Sellers' business card

In 1918 James Thomas Sellers and his wife moved into a house at Railway Terrace. He worked for a time as foreman in the knitting department at Longbottom Mill but his passion was photography. He took many of the photographs of Calderdale which are now seen displayed throughout the area in pubs and clubs.[26] He recorded local scenes, club committees, football teams, cricket teams, family groups and events such as annual galas. Sometimes he would make his photographs into lantern slides and show them on Saturday evenings in his church hall at St Walburga's where people could have the pleasure of seeing themselves on a big screen.

In 1928 he was employed by Lilywhites as their "local view photographer" and he travelled the British Isles taking photos until the start of the war when such activities were no longer allowed. He also played the piano in local pubs and clubs, including the Woodman Inn. When the Salvation Army girl came in with "The War Cry" and "Young Soldier" he would strike up with "The Old Rugged Cross" and insist on her singing it before she was allowed to sell her papers.[27]

40. The Woodman Inn, Luddenden Foot.

Villagers in Luddenden Foot had a sense of belonging to a community and there were sporting rivalries between them and other villages. One of the games associated with local pubs was knurr and spel. Tim Helliwell who was a member of the Co-op committee when it celebrated its fifty-year jubilee in 1910[28] was also a local knurr and spel champion. The game was played in the field besides the King's Arms at Boulder Clough[29] and also on Holmes Park in the village. It has been described as "poor man's golf" because no expensive equipment was needed. The knurr was a long cane with a hardwood block end and the spel was a white dobby a little smaller than a golf ball. When Tim Helliwell played the spel was put in a cup on the block end of the knurr, thrown up in the air and hit as far as possible across the field. The person who hit it the furthest was the winner. It was a skilful game and was taken very seriously, especially as the local bookie was probably there. Twenty pounds a side was not an unusual bet when pub sides were playing, as they would all "chip in" with the money and share any winnings. Later the game was modified slightly and was known as billets. Now the spel, or billet, was placed in equipment on the ground which could be tipped by the foot to lift the ball into the air so that it could be hit. In the late 1940s billets was played in the field at High Lea Green which is where Luddenden Foot now plays cricket.[3031]

According to local cricket historian, Andrew Hardcastle, cricket has been played in Luddenden Foot since the 1860s. In 1862 some matches were played near the railway station in a meadow, owned by the Whitworths and in 1863 the "Luddenden Foot Rising Stars" played a match against the "Luddenden Foot Jolly Boys" in a field owned by W H Thompson who ran the corn mill in Denholme. St Mary's Church at Blackwood Hall, the Methodist Chapel in Denholme and the Friendly Methodist Chapel all had cricket teams. St. Mary's Cricket Club was founded in the 1880s and they played in the Halifax Parish Cup Competitions.[32] In 1888 there was a cricket pitch on the Holmes in the centre of the village opposite Boy Mill.[33] Cricket is still played in the village at High Lee Green although now the club has no church connection. [34]

The Catholic church had a football team, as did some mills including Hellewell's and Fairlea. Mill teams were members of the Workshop Football League and they played teams from other firms in the area.[35] The village football team, Luddenden Foot Association Football Club, played their matches on the Holmes Park pitch.

41. Luddenden Foot AFC 1923-4. Second from the left on the front row is Harry Hellewell, owner of Holme Royd Mill and fourth from the left on the front row is E. E. Cockroft, owner of Fairlea Mill[36]

In September 1923/24, Luddenden Foot won the local cup with a score of 1-0 after five replays. To celebrate the occasion 360 postcards were made of the team and they were sold at 5d each.

A Kershaw Friendship Club member recalled:[37]

"At one time Luddenden Foot boasted the most outstanding amateur football team in the Halifax League. The field, Holmes Park was also the village tip.[38] As the tip grew the playing field was moved forwards until all the space was gone. We then had to find another field until the tip was levelled and re-grassed."

The pubs, clubs and sporting activities were mainly for men. Young women's leisure activities included going to the cinema and dancing but when women were married much of their leisure time would be used sewing, knitting and making clothes for the family. Their duty was to be in the home as wives and mothers.

42. Garden Party in 1924 at Styles Farm, near Finkle Street. Mothers and children.

A Kershaw Friendship Club Member recalled:

"There were six pubs, a British Legion and a Working Men's Club in Luddenden Foot when we were courting before the war. Unfortunately these places were for men only. Women could only visit if they'd been invited into the back room by the landlady. Consequently, our main leisure activity was dancing. There was a dance hall above the Co-op but we sometimes went on an evening trip to The Tower Ballroom, Blackpool. It cost 2/6d by train."[39]

In the 1920s there were council-owned allotments below Belmont Terrace, near Longbottom Mill, which were rented to villagers for 7/6d a year.[40]

The fruit and vegetables grown there would have been welcome in homes experiencing hardship but allotment holders may also have exhibited their blooms at the very popular flower shows that were held on the park. At one well-attended show the police had a very busy time, with a total of six bookies being arrested.[41]

In summer, on the park, there was an annual Luddenden Foot and District Music Festival. In 1930 money raised was in aid of The Royal Halifax Infirmary and hymns and choruses were sung by united choirs of the district assisted by a local brass band. On these occasions the National Anthem was always the final item.[42] The local brass band was based at Friendly and in 1935 they were given a new wooden building for their practice room which was in the field opposite the Friendly pub.[43]

43. Luddenden Foot Boy Scouts. Taken on the canal bank near Longbottom's Mill.

Land in the Holmes was "set apart" by County Councillor Sam Dugdale to provide recreational spaces for children[44] and a recreation ground was formally opened by Mrs Sam Dugdale in May 1924. In 1932 B. W. Clay donated the entrance and park gates, which sadly are no longer there, in 1933 Harry Hellewell donated the open-air shelter and in 1934 J.W. Crossfield provided a drinking fountain. The park was a safe place where village children could play away from the dangers of the road, the river and the canal.

44. Holmes Park, Luddenden Foot, in 1935. The two men are standing by the drinking fountain. The mill chimneys belong to Fairlea Mill and Hellewell's Mill.

45. Holmes park paddling pool. 1930s. Denholme Mill, occupied by the Crossfields, is top centre and the Congregationalist Chapel clock is top right on the horizon.

46. Children at Boys Scarr in the inter-war years. Pictured in front of the sweet shop.

[1] LFUDC minutes, June, July 1921.

[2] LFUDC October 1921.

[3] *Halifax Courier and Guardian*, 20th Feb. 1930.

[4] WYAS MISC:322.

[5] Interview with Cyril Charnley.

[6] Kershaw Friendship Club, *Marbles by Gaslight* (Calderdale Council Leisure Services, 1994).

[7] Milltown Memories 2003-4 Issue 6, 21.

[8] Medical Officer of Health Report, 1925.

[9] Medical Officer of Health Reports.

[10] LFUDC Medical Officer of Health Report1923 WYAS CMT11/MLF39.

[11] Medical Officer of Health Report, 1935.

[12] Kershaw Friendship Club, *Marbles by Gaslight* (Calderdale Council Leisure Services, 1994).

[13] LFUDC minutes, Feb 1915.

[14] LFUDC minutes March 1915 and August 1917.

[15] Kershaw Friendship Club, *Marbles by Gaslight* (Calderdale Council Leisure Services, 1994).

[16] LFUDC Housing Inspection Report, April 1921.

[17] LFUDC minutes, July 1919.

[18] LFUDC minutes, October 1922.

[19] LFUDC minutes, May 1927.

[20] *Victory Souvenir Programme Citizen's Social Wee,k* 1946.

[21] LFUDC Sanitary Inspector's report, March 1932.

[22] Medical Officer of Health Report, 1935.

[23] LFUDC minutes, 1936.

[24] LFUDC minutes, April 1912.

[25] Kershaw Friendship Club, *Marbles by Gaslight* (Calderdale Council Leisure Services, 1994).

[26] Interview with Owen Sellers. His father had a habit of writing in white lettering on the bottom of his photographs.

[27] Owen Sellers, *The Twentieth Century Remembered: Recollections of my Father James Thomas Sellers 1896-1964 Photographer of Luddenden Foot*.

[28] See photograph no. 24.

[29] The "Henpecked Husbands" of Luddenden Foot had their headquarters at the King's Arms at Boulderclough where there was also a Working Men's Club. The club building has been converted into houses.

[30] Interview with Cyril Charnley.

[31] Interview with Lesley Helliwell.

[32] *Halifax Evening Courier*, Sat. 7 July 2007.

[33] O S Map 1888-93.

[34] www.ckcricketheritage.org.uk/caderdale/luddendenfoot/clubhome

[35] Interview with Mary Charnley.

[36] Interview with Owen Sellers.

[37] Kershaw Friendship Club, *Marbles by Gaslight* (Calderdale Council Leisure Services, 1994).

[38] Rubbish was also tipped at Daisy Bank.

[39] Kershaw Friendship Club, *Marbles by Gaslight* (Calderdale Council Leisure Services, 1994).

[40] LFUDC minutes, January 1920.

[41] "Luddenden Foot File", Halifax Central Library.

[42] WYAS 1284/4/4.

[43] LFUDC minutes, June 1935.

[44] LFUDC minutes, July 1917, May 1921.

Chapter 7
Luddenden Foot's war effort

No doubt many villagers heard of the outbreak of war by listening to their wireless sets. My family lived in Luddenden Foot at the time. My grandmother was a feisty woman and my mother told me that she only ever saw her cry once and that was when war was declared in September 1939. Her husband had served in the 1914-18 war and she knew that her son would be called to serve in this one.

Luddenden Foot worked hard for the war effort and activities were recorded in the "Our Village" section of the Victory Souvenir Programme for the "Citizen's Social Week", 1946.

Defence

The Luddenden Foot section of the West Riding Constabulary was trained in civil defence but when they were off duty some of the men formed a glee party to entertain people and in 1942 they organised The Prisoner of War Fund. In four years they raised a total of £1,201 11s 11d, which included £750 0s 1d from "Citizen's Social Weeks".

47. Special Constables in Luddenden Foot. My grandfather, Arthur Butterworth, is seated front on the right

To help out the police during the war, men in reserved occupations or with medical conditions which precluded them from active service, or men who were too old to serve in the forces, were recruited as Special Constables. My grandfather fell into the last category. In the First World War, when he was between the ages of nineteen and twenty-one, he served in the trenches as a stretcher-bearer for two years until 1917 when he was wounded.

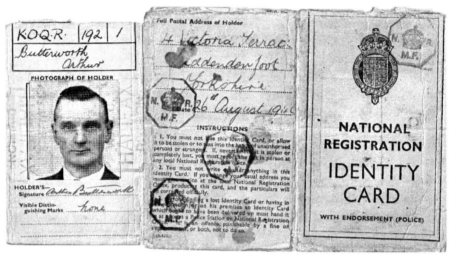

48, 49. Special Constable Identity Card

The ARP (Air Raid Protection) was set up in 1938. When war was declared the ARP headquarters were in a cellar at Dale View. Air Raid Wardens were responsible for: recording the members of each household, distributing gas masks, understanding poison gases and the different types of bombs and organising first aid. They also had to train street groups in the use of stirrup pumps. In Luddenden Foot there were six female wardens and 15 male wardens.

50. Notes made by Air Raid Warden Sellers about how to handle an incident. Dated October 1943.

Guard was formed in May 1940 with its headquarters at the British Legion premises. Within a month the platoon was 40 strong and at one time it had 102 volunteers. At first, all they had were a few shotguns but gradually they became suitably equipped and received training in modern weaponry. One of their duties was to man the observation post at Crow Hill from dusk till dawn.

Stuart Holland in his letter to the *Halifax Courier* in August 1992 remembers a barricade at Bar Wood. He said: "It was put up in the early days of the war when there was a real fear of invasion and it extended well into the middle of the road. There were slots in the road to put in steel girders so that the road could be completely closed. After the initial invasion threat was over the barrier was reduced in size." He went on to say that as kids they used to lie on top of the barricade watching the Home Guard practising putting in the girders.

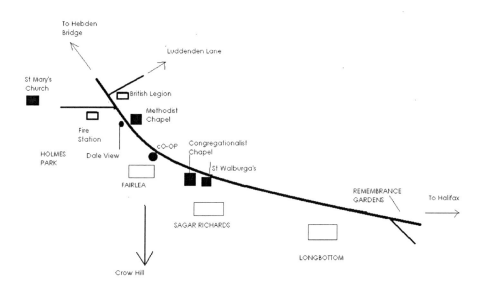

The village had a part-time voluntary fire service and the fire station was near the entrance to the park. In 1939 there were twenty-six firemen and they had one large trailer pump, one light trailer pump and towing vehicles. Part of their duties was to stand by for movement into towns which were being raided by the Luftwaffe, and on one such occasion in December 1940 the Luddenden Foot crew were ordered to Bolton. From there they travelled to Salford on the way passing "hundreds of fires, debris on the roads and continual falling bombs". They were in Salford on duty for about two days, without rest and practically without food. After nights on duty the men would report to their usual employment the following day.

Women's roles

During the war, food rations were shared out to housewives from shops which were understaffed because of "call-ups". Women did a lot of queuing, which may seem trivial but it was done on a daily basis. Often women would join queues outside shops even if they didn't know what was on offer in the hope of being able to take something home for their family.

A Kershaw Friendship Club member recalled:[1]

"A certain grocer used to dabble in the black market. He had dripping all through the war! People used to queue for it! They came for years after the war because he'd been so obliging. He finally had to do a moonlight!"

As well as taking care of their own children, some women in Luddenden Foot took care of evacuees and these children were kept safely in the village throughout the war.

Women organised "The Red Cross Penny a Week Fund" which was a weekly house-to-house collection and the total collected during the war was £623 4s 3d. They set up the Comforts Fund, and in total 3,100 items of clothing, including socks, gloves and pullovers, were knitted and sent out to occupied countries, Red Cross hospitals, the Merchant Navy, and to all villagers who were members of the armed forces. Each person on the Comforts register received two gifts every year and "thank you letters" were sent home:

"Thank you so much for the two parcels of cigarettes, received almost together, both were in good order after travelling half way around the world."

"I wish to thank you for the 15/- postal order just received – and how I appreciate your gift. My case is more outstanding than the rest because before I met my wife I had never heard of Luddenden Foot, and the way you have treated me is simply great."[2]

Local firms

During the war, Sagar Richards, which had started as a small firm by the gas-works at Wood Bottom, moved into the spinning sheds on the other side of the river at Cooper House Mill. The sheds were cleared and equipped for engineering work but Sagar Richards eventually demolished the mill and rebuilt it.

As a youth Lesley Helliwell[3] worked at Sagar Richards and when he started they were making parts for the nozzles of service gas masks. They went on to make parts for tank gearboxes and tank turrets as well as making parts for Bedford trucks which were used by the army. The hot foundry work, casting, was done by men and then the parts went to be machined in the machine shop where half the workforce was made up of women. The women came mostly from the village but some came from further afield.

A Kershaw Friendship Club member recalled:

"I worked at Sagar Richards, making gas mask parts – the bit that went inside to filter the gas. I'd file them, get them passed and then they went elsewhere to be put in the finished mask. We worked stood up all day and it was very tiring. I had young children, so shared shifts with a neighbour. Days started at 6am to 2pm, then 2pm to 10pm, rushing home to swap over looking after the children. I got £2. 0s. 5d a week."

Fairlea Mill wove cotton sheets but during the war they also wove herringbone cloths on narrow looms for use by the navy as gun cleaning cloths.[4]

At Whitworth's Longbottom Mill normal business was producing woollen blankets but during the war they produced cloth for army and RAF uniforms. [5]

51. Taken around 1940 at Luddenden Foot railway station and showing porter Mrs Mary Calvert who was the first woman to replace male employees who had been "called up." Porter Roy Schofield is on the left and on the right is Lloyd Greenwood, later Hebden Bridge Station Master, who started work at the station as a clerk when he was fifteen.

Social Life

After work and war duties were done, village social life continued and the churches and chapels and the Co-op Hall were centres of activity. Wakes Week, the local holiday week, during the war was in August and for people who would be staying at home there were special events. In 1943 these included Punch and Judy shows, magic shows, talent spotting competitions, bowling competitions, mannequin parades, ventriloquists, music by the Sowerby Bridge Home Guard band and dancing.[6]

The old people were not forgotten and the old folks' treat continued although the menu was reduced because of rationing. The tea was ox tongue, boiled ham, pickles, brown and white bread followed by fancy cakes.

In 1941 the guest speaker at the treat was Councillor F. J. Mitchell, JP who was chair of Sowerby Bridge Urban District Council. In 1937 the Luddenden Foot District had lost its administrative independence when it was merged with Sowerby Bridge Urban District Council. This was a state of affairs which may not have been received with overwhelming approval and delight by many Luddenden Footers. In his speech the councillor expressed pleasure at being invited and added "a number of persons had said that there had not been much of a fraternal spirit between Sowerby Bridge and the outside districts since the amalgamation took place about four years ago." He went on "that if it were not possible to get Luddenden Foot and Midgley to go to Sowerby Bridge then he would try to bring a little of the spirit of Sowerby Bridge to the outside districts."

In 1942 the treat continued because the village was reluctant to allow the custom to lapse, especially as it was now the oldest of its kind in the Calder Valley. Because of rationing there were no oranges as gifts and no tea: instead each guest was given a shilling.

In 1943 when local man William Spencer died he had been on the old folks' treat committee for fifty years. He left two 3 per cent Defence Bonds of £5 each to the committee to form the nucleus of an endowment fund to ensure the future of the treats. The fund was called The Spencer Fund[7].

Celebration

When the war was over, the villagers held their fourth Citizens Social Week and published their Victory Souvenir Programme. The whole village was involved in what was a fund-raising event for the Nursing Institution, the Comforts fund, the British Legion, and the Royal Halifax Infirmary. There was no shortage of talent. On Monday evening 4th March there was a concert, given by the workers of the district, in the Congregationalist schoolroom, entitled "Workers' Playtime". On Tuesday evening the Congregationalists presented an operetta entitled "Peach Blossom". Wednesday evening was spent with the Walburgan players who presented a comedy in three acts entitled "Living Room". The Methodists presented the famous Kingsway Singers on Thursday evening and on the Friday evening St Mary's Church presented their children in the pantomime "Cinderella" with their men presenting variety acts. Admission to all these events was 1/6d. Saturday afternoon was for children and at St Walburga's there was film show called "Northern Frontier" which was about the Canadian Mounted Police. Admission was 6d. On the Saturday evening at the Co-operative Hall, the British Legion presented Harry Schofield and his Criterion Dance Band in Old Time Dancing and there was also a whist drive. Admission was 2/-. Sunday saw the Grand Finale Celebrity Concert, "A Fantasy of Song", and admission was 2/6d.

VICTORY SOUVENIR
PROGRAMME

LUDDENDENFOOT
"Citizens' Social Week"
(FOURTH YEAR)

MARCH 4th to 10th, 1946
IN THE
CO-OPERATIVE HALL

＊

PROCEEDS IN AID OF
LUDDENDENFOOT NURSING INSTITUTION
LUDDENDENFOOT COMFORTS FUND
(Registered under The War Charities Act of 1940)
LUDDENDENFOOT BRITISH LEGION REHABILITATION FUND
ROYAL HALIFAX INFIRMARY

＊

PROGRAMME · SIXPENCE

52. Luddenden Foot's Victory Souvenir Programme

During the Second World War four hundred and sixty-seven men and women from Luddenden Foot were drafted into the forces. Twenty-two men were killed, ten men were wounded, and eight men were taken prisoner, six in German hands and two in Japanese hands.

---

1 Kershaw Friendship Club, *Marbles by Gaslight* (Calderdale Council Leisure Services 1994).

2 Both unsigned letters quoted in the Souvenir programme.

3 Interview with Lesley. Helliwell.

[4] Interview with Mary Charnley

[5] Interview with Mary Charnley.

[6] Peter Thomas, *Seeing It Through. Halifax and Calderdale during the War* (2005).

[7] WYAS SPL222-231.

Chapter 8
The Clearances

The Welfare State

In the 1840s people in Calderdale were in despair and they were hungry. Because they feared the workhouse, many tried to protect themselves against hard times by joining a Friendly Society. In the 1940s, after the war, the government was to transform the lives of vulnerable people. There was now to be a Welfare State where the government would be the nation's Friendly Society. Working people would pay regular National Insurance contributions in exchange for free medical care, sick pay, unemployment pay, maternity benefits, child allowances, and a retirement pension at sixty-five for men and sixty for women.

The chapels and churches

Disillusioned by two World Wars and armed with increased education, people were challenging religious beliefs. Services were no longer well-attended but the chapels and churches remained at the centre of village social life, providing leisure activities and working with the village's young people. At the Congregationalist Chapel there were Saturday night concerts, socials and whist drives and for many years a pantomime was produced to which the whole village was invited. Ronnie Baines ran the Boys' Brigade there but it wasn't just for Chapel people, Catholic lads also joined.[1] Children at the chapel enjoyed the annual Sunday school treat which was usually a picnic in the countryside.

Next door, at the Catholic church, the cinema in the basement had been replaced by a dance floor and dances held there included the St Patrick's Ball. They also had a talented amateur dramatics society, The Walburgan Amateur Players, but not all the players were members of the Catholic church, everyone was welcome to join.[2]

53. Saint Walburga's Amateur Dramatic Society Production

The old folks' treat ended

A tradition that continued into the 1950s and '60s was the old folks' treat at the Congregationalist Chapel. Started by John Whitworth's charity, it was now supported by the whole community. Money for the treat was partly raised by a door-to-door collection, and speaking about the collection, Stanley Dugdale, one of the treat's organisers, said: "We don't get many refusals."

1953 was Coronation year and as a special celebration the old folks were taken on a trip to the seaside. A hundred and ninety-one people set off on a specially chartered train to Southport to spend a day in the sun and take high tea before returning home with gifts.

1959 was the centenary year of the treat, which had never missed a year, and on this occasion two hundred people boarded the Leeds to Liverpool express, which stopped specially at the village station. They were taken to Liverpool and then through the Mersey Tunnel to New Brighton.

In the '60s the treat became a lunch and a coach outing to places such as Manchester Airport and Belle Vue. But in 1969 what was now believed to be one of the oldest treats of its kind in the country came to an end. The village had been cleared and now many of the old folks lived on the Kershaw House estate which was part of Luddenden. The money which the treat organisers were left with was given to the Luddenden Foot Forget-me-not Club.[3]

The Mechanics' Institute closed

In 1957 the Mechanics' Institute was discontinued because of lack of interest and a shortage of money. The building was handed over to the council and became known as the Civic Centre.[4] When the Institute closed, Herbert Thomas, who'd had a long association with the Institute, said, "At times it has been a struggle to keep going but in view of the good work done for the young men of the village, the struggle has been well worth while." H.W. Harwood[5] paid tribute to Herbert Thomas, who was an old student of Warley Grammar School. He said, "... after a dozen years as headmaster of Knowle Green, Longridge, near Preston, he came to Luddenden Foot to continue a coal, hay and straw business which was in the family. His voluntary work in education, his long service with Luddendenfoot Congregationalist Church, his love of music and kindly influence are well remembered."

Various organisations met at the Civic Centre in the '50s and '60s, including: the British Legion, the Oddfellows, the Labour Party, the Society for the Blind, the Forget-me-not Club and the Luddenden Foot Association Football Club. The building housed the Child Welfare Centre and the village library, which would later move into rooms in the Victoria Hotel building. Rooms at the Centre were also used for wedding receptions, funeral teas, whist drives and private parties.[6]

The Slipper Baths closed

By 1966 because of falling demand the slipper baths were no longer open on Saturday afternoons and in 1969 they were converted into showers for the use of the local football teams.

54. Luddenden Foot village when there were no concerns about road safety

Luddenden Foot had problems

In Luddenden Foot the standard of housing was poor and many of its houses were alongside Burnley Road, the A646, and as the road became busier, concerns about road safety grew.

Improving the nation's housing stock had been put on hold until after the Second World War when there was a national house-building programme. In March 1947, land above the village, near Kershaw House, was selected as the place to build council houses and it was bought by Sowerby Bridge Council. In April 1948, approval was received from the Ministry of Housing to build 60 dwellings, which were to be 24 houses and three blocks of 12 flats.[7] By September 1952 the first 18 of these houses were offered to applicants and by February 1953 all the houses were available. The council then set about buying more land at Kershaw House because "there was a need to anticipate the future needs of people who would be displaced from unhealthy or dilapidated houses."

Some houses in Luddenden Foot could be improved. In 1955 it had been agreed by the government that improvement grants would be available for "back-to-back" houses where it could be shown that each room would have adequate ventilation.[8] Other houses were considered by the council to be unfit for human habitation and not capable of being made fit at reasonable cost. It was decided that the most satisfactory way of dealing with these houses was to demolish them and In January 1958 house clearances in Luddenden Foot began. Over a period of ten years many houses, including all those on one side of Burnley Road, were demolished. The clearances were to affect about four hundred people.

In January 1958 it was decided that houses at Narrow Neck, Milner Gate, Bottoms Cottages, and Mill Gate would be cleared.[9]

In January 1959 it was decided that three cottages at Butts Green, where four people lived, would be cleared.[10]

In October 1960 it was decided that houses at Woodman Buildings, Denholme Buildings and other properties in Burnley Road, where seventy people lived, would be cleared. [11]

In November 1962 it was decided that Co-operative Buildings, Black Lion Buildings, Brick Buildings, Duke Street and part of Tillotson Buildings, where a hundred and twenty three people lived would be cleared.[12]

In May 1963 it was decided that Lane Side and houses at Blackwood Hall, including some at Booth House, where sixty-one people lived would be cleared. [13]

In March 1966 it was decided that houses at Milner Royd and Albion Terrace, Blackwood Hall, where seventy-five people lived, would be cleared.[14]

In October 1968 it was decided that houses at Robertshaw Buildings, where two people lived would be cleared.[15]

In October 1969 several houses in Bank Buildings were empty and likely to become derelict and it was decided that demolition was the best solution.[16]

In March 1971 it was decided that houses at Turner Buildings would be cleared.[17]

Houses at Osborne Terrace, Blackwood Hall, where forty-four people lived, were cleared and houses at Railway Terrace were cleared.

Clearance Areas in Luddenden Foot

1. Narrow Neck
2. Mill Gate Cottages
3. Butts Green Cottages
4. Woodman Buildings, Bank Buildings
5. Tillotson Buildings
6. Denholme Buildings, Co-operative Buildings, Black Lion Buildings
7. Brick Buildings
8. Duke Street, Mill Lane
9. Property at Booth House, Blackwood Hall
10. Osborne Terrace, Blackwood Hall
11. Albion Terrace, Blackwood Hall
12. Railway Terrace
13. Milner Royd
14. Robertshaw Buildings

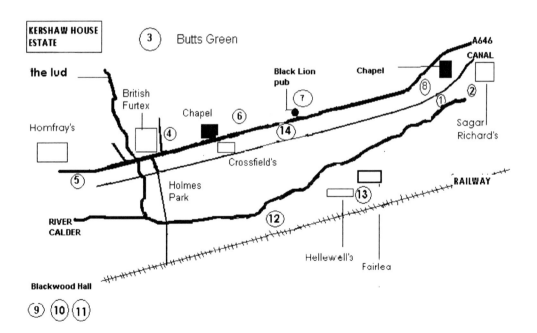

55. Houses were cleared along the length of one side of Burnley Road as far up as the Black Lion pub. The Victoria Hotel Building, which now houses the Post Office, is on the right. 2010

Shops, including the Co-op, closed

The Co-op was still active in the 1950s and there were Saturday night dances in the Co-op Hall. But the Co-op was struggling and Luddenden Foot Co-op was taken over by Sowerby Bridge Co-op in 1964/5. Sowerby Bridge went into administration in 1969 and Luddenden Foot Co-op was closed and later demolished.[18] As the clearances, which included shops as well as houses, progressed, the population of the village decreased. This together with changing shopping habits, because of the arrival of supermarkets, meant that other shops closures followed.

A member of Kershaw Friendship Club said: [19]

"They have pulled down most of the shops that occupied one side of the road. You used to be able to get anything you needed in the Foot. There were plenty of fish and chip shops ... There were several grocers and greengrocers, butchers, confectioners and sweetshops. You could buy a wireless at Kershaw's, clothes at Jackson's or the Co-op, shoes at John Willie Summerscale's, pots and pans at Gilboy's and furniture at

Wilkinson's. There were painters and decorators, plumbers and builders and several undertakers ... We also had a bank, a chemist and a garage. There were several hairdressers."

Another club member said that when Luddenden Foot was thriving, "A conservative estimate would put the number of shops at sixty plus."[20]

In January 1967 one shopkeeper in the village complained to the council of "the adverse circumstances in which they were placed because of the 'blight' placed on the district through housing activities and their consequent inability to dispose of their business."[21]

Road Safety Problems

In the 1950s much energy was directed at educating people about road safety especially children, and there were: road safety exhibitions, "spot the causes" competitions, posters, bookmarks, drip mats for pubs and car stickers.[22] The main traffic troublespot was in the centre of the village where there were: two road junctions (Station Road and Luddenden Lane both joined Burnley Road), a bus stop, a pedestrian crossing, the loading and unloading of wagons belonging to British Furtex (which caused pedestrians to walk into the road) and car parking issues. There was also danger to pedestrians because of the speed at which traffic passed through the village.

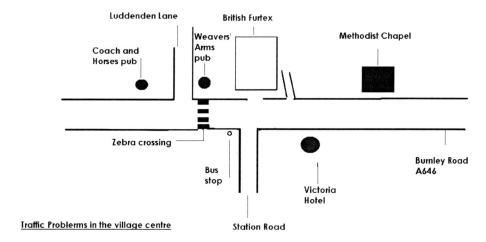

Traffic Problems in the village centre

Road improvements in Luddenden Foot

Sowerby Bridge Council was searching for solutions to the road safety problems in the village. There was speculation about a road-widening scheme but in the early 1970s the traffic problems in the centre of the village were eased in a number of ways. The bus stop was moved into a lay-by on the other side of Station Road next to the Victoria Hotel building. By September 1973 plans were in hand to convert the pedestrian crossing into a Pelican crossing. There were to be peak hour restrictions on the loading and unloading of British Furtex wagons on the main trunk road. Waiting restrictions were planned in Luddenden Lane and Station Road and a 40mph speed limit was introduced between Friendly and Naylor Lane.

In addition to local measures the M62 motorway opened on 14 March 1971 and offered an alternative route across the Pennines for traffic which otherwise may have passed through the village.

The railway station closed

Road transport was increasing and the railways were suffering. In February 1962, because of the decline in numbers of passengers, there was a proposal to withdraw passenger facilities at Luddenden Foot railway station. There were protests but in the September of that year British Rail did withdraw the service and Luddenden Foot railway station closed on the 10th September 1962 as part of the Beeching cuts.

Chapels and churches closed

In February 1959 the trustees of Butts Green Chapel requested its demolition.

By 1965 Denholme Methodist Chapel and Sunday school had closed and their war memorials had been removed and installed at the Civic Centre. The chapel was demolished in 1973.

St Mary's Church of England at Blackwood Hall, Luddenden Foot's parish church, has been demolished and only the graveyard remains. The church closed in its centenary year, 1973. The 126-foot tower was unsafe, there was subsidence and congregations had dwindled. The church organ, which had been installed in 1882, was dismantled and shipped to Japan to be rebuilt there in an Anglican Church. In Japan pipe organs were in great demand and what would have cost around £50,000 to build was obtained by them for a fraction of the price.[23] The National School is now private housing.

St Walburga's Catholic Church was also demolished and on its footprint the St John of God Respite Care Home was opened in 1997.

The clock has stopped at the Congregationalist Chapel. The last service was held there in the June of 2000.[24] The building is standing and has been adapted for re-use as residences. The Congregationalists and Methodists, now joined together as The United Reformed Church, meet in the Civic Centre.

Mills closed

The demolition of the nineteenth-century housing was only part of Luddenden Foot's decline. The village had been a workhorse of the industrial revolution and its work was done.

Carpet manufacturers Homfray's had been running down Delph Mill since April 1970 and it finally closed in November of that year. The mill had employed 95 people but most had found other employment. After the closure, much of Homfray's woollen spinning was done at Prospect Mill, Sowerby Bridge.[25] The footprint of Delph mill is still visible as an empty site next to the Coach and Horses pub, which is now boarded up.

Hellewell's Holme Royd mill, brought down by competition from abroad, closed in 1972 and was demolished. Owen Sellers, then factory manager, said that Harry Hellewell, on his return from the Wool Exchange at Bradford, showed him a package of white worsted yarn from Japan and said, "I bought this for 16/- a pound and I'm trying to sell ours at 18/- a pound."[26] A caravan storage site now occupies the footprint of Hellewell's mill.

Fairlea Mill, spinners and weavers of cotton and waste fabrics, was taken over in 1965 by the Ashton Brothers, who were taken over by Courtaulds in 1968. The mill closed in 1982, another victim of rising costs and falling prices.[27] Calder Valley Auctioneers now occupy part of the mill and the former mill offices. A scrap yard sits on the rest of the footprint of the mill.

56. Tenterfields Business Park, where many of Longbottom's Mill buildings survive, is in the foreground. Along the bottom of the valley, around from Tenterfields and below the clock, is the once Sagar Richard's site, which was formerly the site of Cooper House Mill. The modern Kershaw House Estate is shown on the hillside beyond and to the right of the village. 2010

The former woollen mill at Longbottom is now Tenterfields Business Park. The mill yard and some of the original buildings, including the office block and the weaving sheds, are still there.

Denholme Mill, previously run by the Crossfield brothers, was sold in the 1980s to William Rawsley Ltd., Textile Waste Processors, but it was bought from them in 1992 to be reopened as a camping shop.

British Furtex, the huge mill which stood at the foot of the Lud on the footprint of Foxcroft's fulling mill, was demolished in 2004 and now a housing development occupies the site.

Sagar Richards, employing about 300 people, remained a major employer in Luddenden Foot making parts for car gearboxes. Now the business is run by VTL Automotives who employ 55 men and they also make gearbox parts.

Luddenden Foot – the years between 1952 and 2004

1952	The first houses occupied at Kershaw House Estate
1957	The Mechanics' Institute closed
1958	<u>House clearances begin</u>
1959	Trustees requested the demolition of Butts Green Chapel
1962	The railway station closed (demolished)
1969	The last Old Folks' Treat
	The Co-op closed (demolished)
	The Slipper Baths closed – became showers for sports team
1970	Homfray's Delph Mill closed (demolished)
1972	Hellewell's Mill closed (demolished)
1973	<u>House clearances end</u>
	Denholme Methodist Chapel demolished (closed in 1965)
	St. Mary's Church of England closed (demolished)
1982	Former Fairlea Mill closed (demolished)
1992	Former Crossfield's Mill reopened as a camping shop
1996	Respite Care Home opened on the footprint of St. Walburga's Church
2000	The last service at the Congregationalist Chapel
2004	British Furtex closed (demolished)

---

[1] Interview with Elsie Helliwell.

[2] Interview with Elsie Helliwell.

[3] WYAS SPL 222-231.

[4] SBUDC records, May 1957.

[5] Harwood,"Warley Grammar School", *Trans. Halifax Antiq. Soc.* Jan. 1967.

[6] SBUDC records, Jan. 1958.

[7] SBUDC minutes, December 1948.

[8] SBUDC Housing Committee 19th December 1955.

[9] SBUDC minutes, Jan 1958.

[10] SBUDC minutes, Jan 1959.

[11] SBUDC minutes, Oct 1960.

[12] SBUDC minutes, Nov 1962.

[13] SBUDC minutes, May 1963.

[14] SBUDC minutes, March 1966.

[15] SBUDC minutes, Oct 1968.

[16] SBUDC minutes, Oct 1969.

[17] SBUDC minutes, March 1971.

[18] Robert Huck. (Grocery Dept. Manager at Central Store, Luddenden Foot Co-op. 1960 to 1964/5).

[19] Kershaw Friendship Club, *Marbles by Gaslight* (Calderdale Council Leisure Services 1994).

[20] Estimates vary.

[21] SBUDC minutes, January 1967.

[22] SBUDC minutes, Accident Prevention Committee Report, 1952.

[23] *Halifax Evening Courier*, 13 April 1978.

[24] WYAS GB203 LFC.

[25] *Halifax Evening Courier*, 4 May 1974, "Mill at Luddenden Foot now silent".

[26] Owen Sellers, *Twentieth Century Remembered* - "Recollections of my Father".

[27] WYAS YWC: 1133.

Chapter 9
Towards the Future

Luddenden Foot was a community of decent, hardworking people. When my mother left school she worked at the Co-op in the village but, probably to earn more money, she later worked in local mills including Longbottom's and Fairlea. My father, an off-comer from the Scottish Borders, also spent time at Longbottom's but went on to spend many years as a motor mechanic at Pye Nest garage, Sowerby Bridge.

I was born, in the late 1940s, at Robertshaw Buildings in Luddenden Foot but in the early '50s my family moved to Victoria Terrace in the top o'Denholme area. We escaped the clearances and I lived there until I was eighteen. Home was a back-to-back terraced house with an outside toilet block. Grandparents lived around the back and uncle, auntie and cousins lived just across the valley at Finkle Street. Because over the years people had worked locally and found jobs for their children in the village, there were many extended families in Luddenden Foot. My mother's generation went to school together, worked together, lived as neighbours, raised their children together and grew older together. Often shared experiences made them life-long friends. But sadly, a community that had been built up over many generations was soon to break down.

57. The ladies of the burling department at Whitworth's Longbottom Mill holding their Easter bonnet competition. Taken in the mill yard.

I went to the school across the road from Victoria Terrace and my school friends were also my after-school playmates. One of the things I remember about school is my Yorkshire Penny Bank book and when my parents could afford it I would take small amounts of money to save in my account. Thrift was still being encouraged amongst the working classes.

On Friday evenings or Saturday mornings, to save working mothers' time, local shops would deliver the weekend shopping. The small block of buildings which is still standing across the road and a little way down from the Black Lion pub used to house two shops: Walsh's grocers and Ashworth's butchers, and these shops delivered our family's weekend shopping. My brother's Saturday job was to deliver meat orders for Ashworth's butchers. My mother also shopped at the Co-op and Greenwood was right – divi day was always welcome!

58. Staff at Luddenden Foot Co-op in the 1950s. Elsie Helliwell is front left. She started work in the office at the Co-op in 1943

When I was in my late teens my mother and father would spend Saturday night at the Black Lion pub and sometimes I would tag along. Saturday nights at the Black Lion were well known for their "sing-songs". I remember happy times there when everyone had to "do a turn". I particularly remember that the Irish told the funniest stories.

On Sundays I went to the Congregationalist Chapel and occasionally I would be allowed to toll the bell at 10.25am to indicate that the service was about to start. Sunday afternoon meant Sunday school and spending time in the room under the chapel which had been used nearly a century before by the half-timers from the mills. There were

Sunday school treats and Saturday night socials with games, dances and suppers. There was also the annual pantomime when Jean Vine would transform the Chapel girls into dancing troupers.

But in the second half of the twentieth century, churches and chapels were losing their influence. The textile mills that had sustained the villagers for a hundred years were closing and large-scale clearances would lay waste to much of the village housing and shops. Times were changing and Luddenden Foot would soon become a forgotten place, an empty place to pass through on the way to Halifax or Hebden Bridge.

Kershaw House Estate

Luddenden Foot lost much of its nineteenth-century housing in the clearances. The aim was to provide people with better housing, enabling them to live healthier lives, and this was achieved by building council houses. Opinions about the clearances will differ but Mrs Mary Charnley[1] told me that people were pleased to be moving to Kershaw House Estate. She said:

"Most people were looking forward to going there because they would have inside toilets and bathrooms."

59. The original houses are at the front of the picture, this side of Luddenden Lane. Mytholmroyd is in the distance.

108

60 The top half of the picture shows Kershaw House Estate in the Luddenden Valley. The bottom half shows the top o'Denholme area of Luddenden Foot village. The school is in the middle to the left of the poplar trees, separated from Rose Place by Burnley Road. The Congregationalist Chapel is in the trees on the extreme left.

The Kershaw House Estate is only ten minutes' walking distance from the centre of Luddenden Foot and the new homes, away from the busy road, were structurally sound, large enough, dry, well ventilated, light, and they each had their own plot of land where children could play.

Over the last forty years the community at Kershaw House has grown and now includes two schools (Woodbank and Luddenden Dene), a Youth Centre, a Health Clinic, a pharmacy and a small supermarket.

Luddenden Foot Village

After much of Luddenden Foot was flattened it seemed to lie wounded and forgotten for many years. But recently there have been signs of recovery.

The Council School has been extended.

In 2009 Holmes Park was furbished with a new play area.

The village still has a Post Office in the Victoria Hotel building and there are three pubs. They are the Black Lion, the Brandy Wine Bar, and the Weaver's Arms, which stands on the footprint of Henry Farrar's fulling mill and was formerly the beer house frequented by Branwell Bronte.

61. Burnley Road Council School. 2010.

Luddenden Foot has a bowling club, and cricket continues to be played at High Lea Green. In the 1990s the canal system was cleaned up and revived as an important leisure resource in Calderdale and canal boats once more pass through the village.

62. "Isabel" travelling towards Luddenden Foot. 2009.

There are new houses and some of them have been built on the land cleared when British Furtex was demolished. Built on the footprint of Foxcroft's water-powered fulling mill, they are appropriately called Mill Stream Drive.

Luddenden Foot Community Association

When the Mechanics' Institute closed, their building was taken over by the council and since then it has been known as the Civic Centre. But for the past five years the Luddenden Foot Community Association, now chaired by Jill Smith-Moorhouse, has been working towards having the building sold to the community. Asset transfer is now in process. They believe that the centre has great potential for the village and the surrounding area as a meeting place for community groups. It is used today by the United Reformed Church, the Women's Institute, the local playgroup, the Boys' Brigade and various sports teams. The building is looking a little shabby and facilities there, particularly the changing-rooms and showers, need updating. Fund-raising events include the yearly "Party in the Park" and in 2009 this attracted around 1,500 people and was particularly successful. The 2010 event was equally enjoyable. The ultimate aim of the Association is to completely modernise the Civic Centre. There are plans for the addition of a glass extension to one corner, a wrap-round balcony and a walkway to overlook Holmes Park. They would also like to introduce some eco-friendly means of heating and lighting the building.

Perhaps the next time the power of the Lud is harnessed it will be to produce electricity!

---

[1] Her family were not affected by the clearances.

Abbreviations

WYAS   West Yorkshire Archive Service
LFBH minutes   Luddenden Foot Board of Health minutes
LFUDC minutes   Luddenden Foot Urban District Council minutes
SBUD   Sowerby Bridge Urban District Council minutes
O. S. Map   Ordnance Survey map
Trans. Halifax Antiq. Soc.
       Transactions of the Halifax Antiquarian Society

Bibliography

Census Returns for the Luddenden Foot area 1841, 1861 and 1871

West Yorkshire Archive Service:
HB 62-77   United Methodist   church
WYC:1219/14 Pedigree of the Whitworth Family
MISC:227   Independent Order of Oddfellows Halifax District History of Loyal Rose Lodge No. 808 Luddenden Foot
CMT11 SPL:176. (1868-80) 177 (1880-91) 178 (1891-96)
       Luddenden Foot Board of Health minutes
SPL 216-221 Luddenden Foot Institute minutes 1886- 1946
SPL 222-231 Luddenden Foot Old Folks' Treat records 1877 – 1969
MISC:322   Henry Sagar Ltd. Cooper House, Luddenden Foot
WYC:1133   Fairlea Mill Co Ltd, Luddenden Foot
T/ED 9-10 178 Luddenden Foot School Board records, 1895-
MISC:322   HJ Homfray and Co Ltd
1284/4/4   Programme for the Luddenden Foot and District Music Festival 1930

Luddenden Foot Urban District Council minutes
 Sowerby Bridge Library
Sowerby Bridge Urban District Council minutes
Sowerby Bridge Library
The Halifax Guardian
The Halifax Courier
Kelly's Directory 1893 West Riding of Yorkshire
Halifax Central Library

Ordnance Survey Maps:
1888 –93 sheet ccxxx   7 LFLBD
1907   sheet ccxxx   11 LFUD
1919   sheet ccxxx   11 LFUD
1933   LFUD

 "Victory Souvenir Programme Luddenden Foot Citizens' Social Week" March 4th to 10th 1946: Privately owned.

Bentley, Phyllis, *The Pennine Weaver* (Cedric Chivers Ltd, 1970).

Berry, James, *The Luddites in Yorkshire (*Dalesman Publishing Co Ltd, Clapham via Lancaster Yorks, 1970*)*.

Breakell, Ruth, *Caring and Sharing. How Pennine people turned want into plenty 1840-1914* (Pennine Heritage Network).

Briggs, Asa, *A Social History of England* (Book Club Associates, 1983).

Croft, Linda, *John Fielden's Todmorden* (Tygerfoot Press, 1994).

Du Maurier Daphne, *The Infernal World of Branwell Bronte* (Virago Press, 2006).

Gaskell, Elizabeth, *Mary Barton* (Vintage, 2008).

Greenwood, Joseph (Secretary), *Jubilee of the Luddenden Foot Industrial Co-operative Society Ltd. Facts and Incidents in the History of the above Society. 1860-1910* (Manchester Co-operative Wholesale Society Ltd Longsight, 1910).

Hanson, T.W., *The Story of Old Halifax* (MTD Rigg Publication, 1993).

Hargreaves, John, *Factory Kings and Slaves 1780-1840* (Pennine Heritage Network).

Hargreaves, John, *Sowerby Bridge in Old Photographs* (Smith Settle, 1994).

Harrison, JFC, *Early Victorian Britain 1832-51* (Fontana Press, 1988).

Hartley, Marie and Ingilby, Joan, *Life and Tradition in West Yorkshire* (London: JM Dent & Sons Ltd 1976).

Holt, Jennifer *Cloth for All: changing patterns of the South Pennines textile industry 1840–1914* (Pennine Heritage Network).

Jennings, Bernard (ed.) & Hebden Bridge WEA, *Pennine Valley A history of Upper Calderdale.* (Smith Settle Ltd. 1992).

Kershaw Friendship Club, *Marbles by Gaslight* (Calderdale Council Leisure Services 1994).

Milltown Memories: Issues 4, 6, 7, and 9.

Reach, Angus Bethune (ed. Chris Aspin), *Fabrics, Filth and Fairy Tents :the Yorkshire Textile Districts in 1849. An Eyewitness account of textile workers' conditions in Huddersfield, Dewsbury, Batley, Halifax, Bradford and Leeds in 1849* (Royd Press 2007).

*The Rochdale Canal (*Waterways Handbook Co. 3, Hillsborough Unsworth, BL98LE*)*.

Sellers, Owen, *The Twentieth Century Remembered:* "Recollections of my Father James Thomas Sellers 1896-1964, Photographer of Luddenden Foot.".

Thomas, Peter, *Seeing It Through: Halifax and Calderdale during the War* (2005)..

The Transactions of the Halifax Antiquarian Society:

Binns, G R, *Water Wheels in the Upper Calder Valley* (1972).

Hallowes, D M, *"Henry Briggs .Mathematician"* (Nov 1961).

Holroyde, H, *Textile Mills Halifax 1770-1851* (1979).

Hargreaves, J, *Halifax and the Yorkshire Luddite Disturbances of 1812.*

Spencer, C, *Child Labour in the Early Textile Mills* (1991).

Harwood, HW, *"Warley Grammar School"* (Jan 1967).

Turner, John Munsey, *Thunderclaps from Heaven: Calderdale's Heritage of Non-conformity* (Metropolitan Borough of Calderdale, 1984).

Unstead, R J, *England, Book 4: A Century of Change 1837–1937* (London: A & C Black Ltd. 1963).

Walvin, James, *Victorian Values* (Andre Deutsch Ltd, 1987).

Webster, Eric, *Textiles and Tools Nineteenth Century Industry in Calderdale* (Eric Webster*).*